The Good News Is
Better Than You Think

THE
GOOD NEWS
IS
BETTER
THAN YOU
THINK

Robert J. Wieland

CFI Book Division
Gordonsville, Tennessee

Bible quotations in this book are from the following versions:

Unless otherwise noted Bible quotations are from *The New King James Version*, Copyright © 1979, 1980, 1982 by Thomas Nelson, Inc.

(NEB) *The New English Bible*, Copyright © The Delegates of the Oxford University Press and The Syndics of the Cambridge University Press, 1961, 1970; Oxford University Press, New York, 1971.

(GNB) *Good News Bible*: The Bible in Today's English Version, Copyright © American Bible Society, 1966, 1971, 1976.

(NIV) *New International Version of The Holy Bible*. Scripture taken from THE HOLY BIBLE, NEW INTERNATIONAL VERSION. Copyright ©1973, 1978,1984 by International Bible Society. Used by permission of Zondervan Publishing House.

(KJV) *King James Version*, Copyright ©1988, B. B. Kirkebride Bible Company, Inc., Indianapolis, IN.

(RSV) *Revised Standard Version*, Copyright © 1952 (Old Testament), 1946 (New Testament) by Division of Christian Education of the National Council of the Churches of Christ in the United States of America; Thomas Nelson & Sons, New York, 1952.

(NASB) *New American Standard Bible*, Copyright © The Lockman Foundation, 1960, 1962, 1963, 1971, 1973, used by permission.

Published by CFI Book Division

P.O. Box 159, Gordonsville, Tennessee 38563

ISBN-10: 0-9975122-4-5
ISBN-13: 978-0-9975122-4-3

Printed in the United States of America

Typeset in 11.5/13.8 Minion Pro

How beautiful upon the **MOUNTAINS** ARE THE FEET of him who brings **GOOD NEWS** WHO PUBLISHES PEACE Isaiah 52.7

CONTENTS

1

You've Got to Learn How to Believe Good News!

(It's easier to believe Bad News because we're born to do so)

L et's state our thesis up front, so our gentle reader may move on if he wants to read another book instead:

- Our idea is striking and controversial: what people have thought is "the gospel" turns out to be much better Good News than most have dared to believe.
- An infiltration of half-concealed Bad News has plagued the Christian church for the better part of two millennia. It paralyzes people spiritually, but they can't figure out why they're so "lukewarm" in their devotion.
- Therefore we must rediscover the original "Good News" idea that permeates the New Testament.

When the gospel took off originally, Christ's apostles were accused of "turning the world upside down" (Acts 17:6). It wasn't their personality or public relations savvy; they had gotten hold of a big idea that was itself revolutionary.

People who heard it reacted in ways that could only be called violence—Jesus Himself said that those who liked it were taking "the kingdom of heaven [by] violence, ... by force" (see Matthew 11:12). That is, when they believed what they heard, they believed explosively—they grabbed it with all the energy they had. There was something in the Good News itself that automatically released them from inhibitions and transformed them into joyous (yes, fearless!) capable communicators of the message.

And Those Who Didn't Like the Idea?

They also became violent—in persecuting those who did like it. Thus you read of Christians being fed to lions in the Roman amphitheaters.

Humanity was catalyzed by this apparently wild idea that the gospel is better good news than humanity could dream up on their own. The Bible was seen as Heaven's up-to-the-minute newspaper, and those who liked the Good News in it couldn't get enough. Their enthusiasm for the "TV" and "videos" of their day vanished overnight (yes, they had their amusements, more powerful than our "sports"—genuine chariot races, gladiator fights, all with free admission). These believers had discovered that God's Good News idea was so intensely interesting that what they had thought was "fun" now became boring, repulsive.

What made the Good News so amazingly good was the discovery of what Christ had accomplished for the human race. It was emphatically not what He had *tried* to accomplish, but what He actually *had done*. They shouted from the housetops: Christ has saved the world! He has redeemed humanity! He has given the gift of salvation to every human soul! "Now, believe it," they said.

But then immediately a problem surfaced: *it wasn't easy for people to believe*. They were so used to believing Bad News that it hurt to start believing Good News. And this problem is what brings us to a look at our thesis.

Although Jesus said that His "yoke is easy, and My burden is light," He didn't mean that it's easy for us human beings to *believe* that His yoke is easy. As we shall see later, it *is* easy to be saved and hard to be lost if we understand and believe how good this Good News is; yet learning to believe it is the only difficult step in following Him.

The reason is that we human beings have been born and nurtured in unbelief. This again is why we are so prone to fear. It's natural for us to *dis*-believe. That's why when He came to save us, Jesus met with such massive unbelief that it led people to crucify Him (if He were to come back again today as He was, the world would crucify Him again). That deep-seated unbelief leads to what is called sin.

Simon and Schuster of New York once published a best-seller (1984) by Ben J. Wattenberg entitled, *The Good News Is the Bad News is Wrong*. It hit a sensitive nerve, for it assured millions that their pessimistic forebodings about our economic, political, and moral pulse were wrong. The "good news" about our nation was much better than they had thought, so the book said.

The news about God's will for your future is far more important. Money and political clout cannot buy a moment's genuine happiness, and happiness is the name of the game. (You remember the Enron executive who had sold his stock for $35 million, yet locked himself in his new Mercedes and shot himself?) The "Good News" we are talking about concerns our personal happiness for now and forever. It fills the heart with joy even if we have to live in poverty, sickness, or loneliness. It's what millionaires want but almost never get.

If we face reality, most of us have nearly given up hope that such happiness is attainable. We expect to live out our days with a nagging undertow of frustration and disappointment, even though a fleeting taste of pleasure at times makes life seem worth living. But the undercurrent surfaces again, and indefinable feelings of depression like a riptide sweep us into despair. Even many youth who never won $35 million try to take their own lives. We need something better than we have heard.

The word "gospel" has the built-in meaning of "good news." "Jesus came ... announcing the Good News about God" (Mark 1:14, *Barclay*). His message majored in paths to happiness. Nine sure-cure prescriptions for it glisten in His Sermon on the Mount, each one beginning, "Happy are those who ..." (Matthew 5:3-12, GNB). You may be surprised to discover that not one tells us what *to do* in order to be "happy," but what *to believe*.

If happiness depends on my doing the right thing, I always run into the snag of not being able to do it right. There is always an element of non-attainment. If God promises me something good dependent on the condition that I first do something right, His promises are sure to fail because I can't perform. God may promise me the sky, but it's a cruel trick if His promises are nullified by an impossible pre-condition.

Have you ever received an official-looking junk-mail letter telling you that you are on the way to winning the jackpot? If God's "good news" is a similar hoax, then He turns out to be the Chief Deceiver on earth. Teen suicides would not be what they are if the kids hadn't inherited from somewhere such an idea.

Why Is It So Difficult for Us to Believe God's Good News?

It's fantastic, phenomenal, the wonder of heavenly angels who watch—how the great bulk of humanity prefer Bad News to Good. When Someone came into our midst bringing us Good News, "we" were so upset that "we" rose up and crucified Him. (Maybe you say, Ah yes, but that was 2000 years ago and those were *bad* people; we are different. We would never do that.)

And here's the root of our problem: we don't understand ourselves. The Bible says we are all the same—by nature. *The New English Bible* renders Romans 3:23 as, "All *alike* have sinned," and that is clearly what Paul says for in 8:7 he adds, "The carnal mind is enmity against God." That "carnal mind" is standard DNA equipment for "all" of us, none "exempted" from that universal inheritance, not even the Virgin Mary. All humans are born in a state of separation from God; we have to *learn how* to believe Good News (Mary learned!). We can claim no superiority of virtue over those people of 2000 years ago. In a corporate sense, "they" were "we."

We cannot believe what Jesus says unless we believe that His "yoke is easy" and His "burden is light." But for sure, honest common sense tells us that *believing* that Good News is not "easy." Continually we human beings, in the church or outside, slide into that groove of unbelief like the Israel who couldn't "enter into" their Promised Land "because of unbelief" (Hebrews 4:6, KJV). Unbelief is still our corporate sin.

Since God has nothing for us but Good News, it's obvious that our proclivity for Bad News must be the result of our being "alienated [from God] and enemies in your mind," so that our sinful "mind is enmity against God" (Colossians 1:21; Romans 8:7, KJV). We are all "like them" "in our natural condition" (Ephesians 2:3, NEB). Until we learn to know who He is, this alienation from God results in "having their understanding darkened, ... because of the hardening of their heart" (Ephesians 4:18). It's due to a wrong idea of God's character. We inherited it ultimately from our pagan forefathers. It weaseled its way into the church—the feeling that God is an enemy to be placated. We must *do something* to be shielded from His "wrath."

Today we say we are safely past that global state of adolescence, but that innate state of fear keeps surfacing. After our terrible "September 11" our modern inventions and comforts seemed powerless to assuage our inner fears. Bad News has us all pretty well hyped. We still wrestle with our fears of cancer, poverty, accidents, terrorism. Surveys have indicated that most American youth think they must die someday in nuclear war just as many youth in the 1930s feared dying in a war with German Nazism (and many did). All this negative angst is in proportion to our emotional distance away from God, which means we are born believing Bad News.

An Enemy Called Satan Is the Source

A stalking cobra can paralyze its fear-crazed, hypnotized victim until it strikes. Believing Bad News paralyzes the human soul. It is a fact that witch doctors in Africa have succeeded in "cursing" helpless victims who then lie down and die for no organic reason. But the Greek of Hebrews 2:14 says that the Savior came to paralyze *that enemy* of our souls "and release those who through fear of death were all their lifetime subject to bondage." When Christ was crucified, the devil was not killed, much to the disappointment of many; *but he was paralyzed.*

An example of how a strong man was paralyzed cobra-like by believing Bad News is King Saul of ancient Israel. Admittedly, he had rebelled against God and done practically everything wrong. His kingdom was in jeopardy and his army dispirited while facing a hostile force of Philistines, far outnumbered. The king had cut off every means by which God wanted to help him, yet God sent him no message of doom. Saul still had the option of repentance.

He chose not to take it, but went to a spiritist medium seeking some idea of what to do. The witch was controlled by Satan and told the horror-stricken king a string of calamities that "the Lord" would inflict upon him to bring him and the nation to ruin. But God Himself sent the king no such message; *Saul believed her Bad News.* Her message crushed out of his soul the last tiny spark of hope. He ended his life by a suicide totally unnecessary (1 Samuel 28, 31).

God has never driven any soul to suicide, no matter how many mistakes he or she may have made. Saul could have repented, acknowledged his many sins, and called the nation to prayer for deliverance. A gracious God would have answered as He has often done. Such humbling of his soul would have been infinitely better than suicide.

No matter how bad you may feel or how hopeless your outlook, the Lord has some good news for you: "*Let* not your heart be troubled; you believe in God, believe also in Me." "Whatever you ask in My name, that I will do. ... If you ask anything in My name, I will do it." "Peace I leave with you, My peace I give to you; not as the world gives do I give to you. *Let* not your heart be troubled, neither let it be afraid" (John 14:1, 13, 14, 27).

Jesus recognized here a profound principle of psychiatry—you cannot be paralyzed by Bad News unless you choose to *dis*-believe Good News. Bad News may come knocking on your door, but it can never get inside your soul until you say, "Come in." "*Let* not your heart be troubled, neither *let* it be afraid," He urges. To "let" means to give your consent. So, to "*let* ... your heart be troubled" means to consent to believe Satan's Bad News. It's your volition.

Genuine truth is always full of hope. For example, we are afraid for the doctor to tell us the dreaded news that we have inoperable cancer, and we want to avoid facing the fact. But we forget so easily that death "in Christ" is far better than living without Him. Losing one's soul is far worse than mere dying. If the Lord permits us to sleep in death, the fact remains that He is still what He has always been—"God is love" (1 John 4:8).

For a person lying on a deathbed, God has nothing but good news. What He wants him or her to understand is the truth of a Savior who died to redeem us from eternal death, and whose resurrection after three days is the pledge that we too will be resurrected to endless life in Him. There is no situation so bad where God has no good news for us. (Even the unpardonable sin against the Holy Spirit is a final, irrevocable choice to *dis*-believe God's Good News, a determined, conclusive resistance of the Holy Spirit (Matthew 12:24-35; Hebrews 6:4-10).

The Most Common Sin of All Mankind

Not believing, *dis*-believing, is what the Bible calls unbelief. It has been the number one sin of the ages. Israel could not enter into their Promised Land "because of unbelief" (Hebrews 4:6, KJV). When Jesus the Great Healer visited His home town Nazareth, "He did not do many mighty works there because of their unbelief" (Matthew 13:58). Their massive unbelief deprived them of great blessings. It was uncanny how the multitude could stand in the presence of the Son of God Himself, and still choose to cherish their Bad News. Jesus "marveled because of their unbelief" (Mark 6:6).

Jesus told His disciples who were stymied in their efforts to heal a desperately sick child that their "unbelief" was the problem (Matthew 17:20). Even after His resurrection, His disciples for a time preferred Bad News to Good, refusing to believe the testimony of eyewitnesses who knew He had risen from the dead. "He rebuked their unbelief and hardness of heart, because they did not believe those who had seen Him after He had risen" (Mark 16:14). Yes, those eleven disciples faced the stiffest test of believing that human beings have ever faced—the good news was so fantastically "impossible" that it seemed more than they could do to believe "He is risen!"

Put yourself in their place. Here you are in the deepest trough of despair you have ever known, your Savior is dead, buried in a tomb; your hopes have been crushed by the most giant bulldozer of all time—the crucifixion. There seems not the faintest glimmer of a ray of light at the end of your tunnel. Now, can you believe the reports of some excitable women like Mary Magdalene who say they saw Him risen from the dead? Think it through. Maybe you will want to kneel down with those "rebuked" disciples and take your share for not believing Good News!

No wonder the writer of Hebrews pleads with us: "Beware, brethren, lest there be in any of you an evil heart of unbelief in departing from the living God; but exhort one another daily, while it is called 'Today,' lest any of you be hardened through the deceitfulness of sin" (3:12, 13).

The best Good News that a confused or despair-battered human being can hear is that this moral and spiritual paralysis is a disease, a sin, that has already been healed in the person of the Son of God—healed in our fallen, sinful flesh. He became one of us, took on Himself our nature, actually identified Himself with our root problem of alienation from God, and He abolished our sin right there.

Thus He established for all humanity a new identity in Himself, irrespective of how bad our sins may be. He has made alienation, sin, and fear, more outmoded than caveman living. Darkness of mind is now passé, something unnecessary. In what Christ accomplished (not just tried to do) human despair has become an anachronism. God and His entire universe of light welcome us as "accepted in the Beloved" Son of God (Ephesians 1:6). It staggers the mind to realize what He *has done.*

"You, who once were alienated and enemies in your minds by wicked works, yet now He has reconciled in the body of His flesh through death, to present you holy, and blameless, and irreproachable in His sight" (Colossians 1:21, 22).

"But," you say, "I'm very reproachable. I feel in my deepest self all kinds of reasons why I deserve 'reproach.'"

Yes, the blemishes and the blame are still there (as they are for the vast billions of human beings everywhere). Nonetheless, Christ's sacrifice in our behalf gives Him the astounding right to "present" us before the Father and His universe as holy in His sight, without blemish and free from accusation. The grand point of this tremendous Good News is simply this: all the sin and darkness and pollution that still oppress us are kept going only by our continued unbelief of His Good News!

When we begin to stretch our soul to believe it, His deliverance begins immediately to be operative in our heart, to produce changes we never thought possible.

Your Personal Notes

A wise man will hear and increase learning, And a man of understanding will attain wise counsel (Proverbs 1:5).

2

Why God's Good News Has Explosive Power

(It's in the message itself)

Why does salvation come through believing Good News rather than doing good works? It's not because of God's arbitrary decision. Good works can't change any human heart. And it's not some obscure theological mystery.

Simple common sense explains it: after you get through doing everything good you can think of, you find that your original selfishness is still intact. It may be disguised so you can hardly recognize it, but history is replete with "religious" people wearing themselves out with good works who do it all for self-centered reasons. However disguised, their real motivation was racking up points for a reward. Genuine love never had a chance to get in. "If I give all I possess to the poor and surrender my body to the flames, but have not love, I gain nothing" (1 Corinthians 13:3, NIV).

Phony good news would tell us that some selfishness is okay because there's no use hoping for a genuine change of heart; it's impossible. Just adjust your thinking. Other people are that way; why not you?

Such counterfeit good news also declares that God Himself will be content for us to go on like we are, so long as we say we "accept" Jesus. He will whitewash us in the final judgment.

Bible Good News Is Better

The clearest chapter about it is the one where Jesus describes being "born again." A member of the highest ruling council, Nicodemus knew that he needed help. His hypocrisy worried him. Coming well after working hours, Nicodemus sought out Jesus "by night" for an interview. He rather awkwardly began the conversation with some faint praise:

"'We know you are a teacher who has come from God, …' In reply Jesus declared, 'I tell you the truth, no one can see the kingdom of God unless he is born again.'

"'How can a man be born when he is old?' Nicodemus asked. 'Surely he cannot enter a second time into his mother's womb to be born!'

"Jesus answered, 'I tell you the truth, no one can enter the kingdom of God unless he is born of water and the Spirit. Flesh gives birth to flesh, but the Spirit gives birth to spirit'" (John 3:2-6, NIV).

Some things Christ said that night were like time bombs sown in Nicodemus's mind. They released their powerful energies as time went on. A better metaphor is that these truths were like flower seeds planted in a desert, seeds that appear to be dead until spring rains and sunshine awaken them to exuberant life.

The point is that these truths have inherent power. The Savior did not tell Nicodemus that *he* must produce his own new birth. The "you-must-be-born-again" was not a do-it-yourself enterprise. Jesus went on to explain the Good News that this miracle is what *the Lord does*, not man. It's discouraging for a person to be told over and over that he "must be born again" when he thinks the job is up to him to perform. No human being has ever "born" himself (excuse me; we need a new verb); he simply had to let his parents do it for him. So, says Jesus, Nicodemus let the Holy Spirit, superseding his parents, perform the new birth within him:

"You should not be surprised at My saying, 'You must be born again.' The wind blows wherever it pleases. You hear its sound, but you cannot tell where it comes from or where it is going. So it is with everyone born of the Spirit" (verses 7, 8, NIV).

The Divine Obstetrician

Surprising as it may seem, the Good News is *very* good: (1) the Holy Spirit does the new-birth work, and (2) He will do it if you don't frustrate Him. (People who love Bad News won't like this.)

That "wind" is forever blowing seeds of heavenly truth into minds and hearts. No one is wise enough to tell where they come from, for the grace of God has been working on human hearts in multitudinous ways ever since time began. What parents have said, friends, songs of praise, Bible messages heard or read, sermons, expressions of true love—all can be ways that the Holy Spirit uses to plant "Good News" ideas in the heart.

These "seeds" may lie there deep, unrecognized for years, but they are certain to germinate because each one has within itself the mysterious principle of eternal life. Each "seed" of Good News truth "is the power of God to salvation" (Romans 1:16).

Here is another illustration of how the divine word of truth accomplishes its purpose:

> As the rain and the snow
>   come down from heaven,
> and do not return to it
>   without watering the earth
> and making it bud and flourish,
>   so that it yields seed for the sower
>   and bread for the eater,
> so is my word that goes out from my mouth:
>   It will not return to me empty,
> but will accomplish what I desire
>   and achieve the purpose for which I sent it.
>   —Isaiah 55:10, 11 (NIV)

Christ's illustration of the wind blowing "wherever it pleases" is a picture of God's compassionate concern for every person. As surely as you have felt the wind blowing on your cheek, so surely is the Holy Spirit trying to convert you. "God does not show favoritism" (Acts 10:34, NIV).

It's exciting, for at times you can almost *feel* those seeds of truth germinating within your soul like a pregnant woman can feel the baby growing within her. She is thrilled with new life forming. What greater joy to experience something even more wonderful—"I'm being born again!"

But if the New Birth Is So Easy, Why Isn't *Everybody* Born Again?

The answer is clear: many, perhaps the majority, practice a form of new-birth abortion. They are endlessly snuffing out the new life that the Spirit of God imparts.

This is disclosed in Stephen's words to the Jewish leaders of his day. They were only doing what comes naturally to unconverted human nature: "You stiff-necked people ...! You are just like your fathers: You always resist the Holy Spirit!" (Acts 7:51, NIV).

It's active alienation or enmity against God. It doesn't make sense to do that, but let's face reality—that's what we do. It's like starving people diligently uprooting every little food-bearing plant that comes up out of the ground. It's crazy!

The Embryonic New Life Is Snuffed Out Before It Can Grow

Jesus told a parable to illustrate the fate that most of His seeds of truth meet.

"A farmer went out to sow his seed. As he was scattering the seed,

[1] Some fell along the path, and the birds came and ate it up.

[2] Some fell on rocky places, where it did not have much soil. It sprang up quickly, because the soil was shallow. But when the sun came up, the plants were scorched, and they withered because they had no root.

[3] Other seed fell among thorns, which grew up and choked the plants" (Matthew 13:3-7, NIV).

He went on to explain His story. The farmer represents Himself, sowing His seeds of "Good News" truth in all human hearts everywhere through the work of the Holy Spirit, the "wind." But, He says, "this people's heart has become calloused; they hardly hear with their ears, and they have closed their eyes" (verse 15, NIV). It's no use sowing seed in earth packed beneath the tread of multitudes in the path. Even if plenty of seeds fall on hard hearts, they cannot take root.

What Jesus Explains Is So Simple a Child Can Easily Grasp It

[1] "When anyone hears the message about the kingdom and does not understand it, the evil one comes and snatches away what was sown in his heart. This is the seed sown along the path.

[2] "The one who received the seed that fell on rocky places is the man who hears the word and at once receives it with joy. But since he has no root, he lasts only a short time. When trouble or persecution comes because of the word, he quickly falls away.

[3] "The one who received the seed that fell among the thorns is the man who hears the word, but the worries of this life and the deceitfulness of wealth choke it, making it unfruitful" (verses 19-22, NIV). So far, it's Bad News.

But wait, *there is* some Good News left in this story:

[4] Some "seed fell on good soil, where it produced a crop—a hundred, sixty or thirty times what was sown." This is "the

man who hears the word and understands it," Jesus explained (Matthew 13:8, 23, NIV). He is the one who *believes* the Good News, who receives it, welcomes it, cherishes it.

He *lets* it get into his heart instead of inviting the birds by the wayside to snatch it up, or letting the thorns choke it out, or leaving hidden "rocks" of cherished lust to dwarf its roots. *He simply does not perform an abortion of unbelief to kill it.* This is a Good News view of Jesus' parable.

No one has yet seen what is the dynamic factor that *produces* the new birth, because love can never be seen. Jesus told Nicodemus in advance the story of His cross, which of course he couldn't understand that night. But what he heard stayed deep in his mind until he saw what happened; then it all came together, and he stepped out of his closet to identify openly with Christ.

No New Birth Would Be Possible Without Seeing and Appreciating What Happened on the Cross

Jesus explained further:

> "No one has ever gone into heaven except the one who came from heaven—the Son of Man. Just as Moses lifted up the snake in the desert, so the Son of Man must be lifted up, that everyone who believes in Him may have eternal life" (John 3:13-15, NIV).

He alludes to something that happened during Israel's wilderness wanderings. The people were journeying through the desert to their Promised Land (yes, there were hardships). But true to form for all of us humans, they had to make their difficulties worse by believing Bad News: "The people grew impatient on the way; they spoke against God and against Moses, and said, 'Why have you brought us up out of Egypt to die in the desert?'" (Numbers 21:4, 5, NIV). They were not about to die, for God was leading them; this was a specter of doom that they themselves invoked, without reason (see Psalm 105:37). Their doubt became pure unbelief, borrowing troubles that were only figments of their faithless imagination. *But to do so was sin.*

Then the Poisonous Snakes Struck

The people's sinful unbelief and murmuring had deprived them of God's special protection which would have been theirs by right. Moses' making a snake of brass and holding it up high on a pole was an acted prophecy of Christ to be uplifted on His cross.

"The Lord said to Moses, 'Make a snake and put it on a pole; anyone who is bitten can look at it and live.' ... Then when anyone was bitten by a snake and looked at the bronze snake, he lived" (Numbers 21:8, 9, NIV).

But how could a poisonous snake represent Him? Here is the answer: He was "made ... to be sin for us, who knew no sin; that we might be made the righteousness of God in Him" (2 Corinthians 5:21, KJV). We see how close Christ has come to us. He never sinned, but He identified with us so closely that He "took" our fallen, sinful nature. He was "made" to be something that He was not. In that reality is our salvation from the "serpents."

Note how easy the healing was: *all the people had to do was look.* Jesus is telling Nicodemus: there is something to *see* on that cross—*look.* But it is more than gazing at a crucifix. "Looking" is believing in the sense of a heart appreciation of what it cost the One who died there to "be made sin for us," and save us. (It meant that He died the death that we have deserved.)

An appreciation of what He did is what brings healing to a sin-sick person. And, of course, healing is exactly the same as that new birth.

Then Jesus spoke the well-known words that have become the most loved verse of the entire Bible: "For God so loved the world that He gave His one and only Son, that whoever believes in Him shall not perish but have eternal life" (John 3:16, NIV).

Obviously, the power is in the One on that cross, not in its wooden beams. How can believing or appreciating God's act of loving and giving do anything to change sinful hearts?

One of Christ's followers made it clear how it worked for him. He expresses it as a principle that operates in everyone who will look and say, "Thank You" for what He accomplished. Paul was defending himself against the charge that his all-out devotion to Christ was virtual insanity (his faith worked like that "violence" that Jesus spoke about in our last chapter). He was going through incredible hardships and persecutions for Christ's sake, but almost incredibly, he sang for joy as he went along.

The idea that *he* was sacrificing anything seems not to have crossed his mind. On and on he went through scourgings (and one lethal stoning!), imprisonments, fastings, cold and nakedness, shipwrecks, hunger, weariness. His career as a missionary went on for decades, even into old age. Why not restrain his self-sacrificing devotion, and settle down and enjoy a well-earned retirement? Wasn't it time for Paul to begin looking out for "number one"?

No, not for him. He says: "If we are beside ourselves, it is for God; or if we are of sound mind, it is for you. For the love of Christ constrains us, because we judge thus: that if One died for all, then all died [that is, all would be dead if He had not died for them; and so closely are we identified with Christ that when He died, we died too]; and He died for all, that those who live should live no longer for themselves, but for Him who died for them and rose again (2 Corinthians 5:13-15).

Here we see what it has seemed impossible to understand. Paul was not a better person than we are, nor more heroic. He simply *saw something* that made all his sacrifices easy:

- He *saw* that he would be in a hopeless grave if that "One" had not died in his place.
- He *saw* that even his next breath he owed to Christ's sacrifice on the cross.
- He *saw* himself a slave bought by love, responding to the blood shed there.
- He *saw* that nothing he possessed he could count as really his.

He could have sung Isaac Watts' hymn:

When I survey the wondrous cross,
On which the Prince of glory died,
My richest gain I count but loss,
And pour contempt on all my pride.

Were the whole realm of nature mine,
That were a tribute far too small;
Love so amazing, so divine,
Demands my life, my soul, my all.

As easily as the believing Israelites were healed of their fatal snake bites, so easily does the new birth occur in the heart of anyone who "sees" the cross like Paul saw it.

Of course, he did not see it literally—he was not one of the original Twelve. He saw it *by faith*, and his experience is therefore an encouragement to us who also have never seen it literally. What he saw by faith seems to have made a more profound impression on him than the actual event made on those apostles who did see it. None of them seems to have caught its meaning as vividly as Paul did. That means something special for us who never saw the physical happening as did the Eleven (a thousand movies can't portray it!). We are especially fortunate because that same *faith-inspired devotion* can be ours. Because

23

of faith, Paul has to be better news than the other apostles! Faith has far sharper discernment than our physical eyes.

Suppose someone looks but does *not* appreciate the sacrifice of Christ? The heart can be hardened by a choice to *dis*-believe which immediately becomes the famous sin of "unbelief." Jesus went on to tell Nicodemus that no one will ever be lost because of his past sins, because Christ already has died and paid their penalty. Our own *dis*-belief sets us up for a do-it-yourself job of judgment:

> "God did not send His Son into the world to condemn the world, but to save the world through Him. Whoever believes in Him is not condemned, but whoever does not believe stands condemned already because he has not believed in the name of God's one and only Son. This is the verdict: Light has come into the world, but men loved darkness instead of light because their deeds were evil" (John 3:17-19, NIV).

Thus everyone's destiny hangs on his heart-response to that cross. The new birth occurs, not by our *doing* this or that impossible assignment, but by simply *looking* with the eye of heartfelt faith at what that "wondrous cross" means. The healing power is in the word itself; it contains the Good News. And it is already yours; it has already been given you "in Him"; don't throw it away.

Let it come into your heart. *Let* it take root. Don't practice abortion on it. Cherish it. Plead with God with all your soul for His gift of faith. He has promised to give you every tiny bit that you are willing to cherish.

There can be no such thing as Bad News unless we ask for it, or choose it, and thus willfully bring on ourselves a final verdict of choosing darkness after we have seen Light.

3

More Good News: God's Love Is Active, Not Passive

(Let's look again: Is the "new birth" hard work?)

We know we need to be changed from the inside out. Years of being what we are have made us set in our ways, we feel. Our problems are a part of us, through and through, whether it's lust, appetite, jealousy, or whatever has a hold on us. How can we become really different than what we are?

We can change the color of our hair, but how can we change the color of our eyes? If we were born to be short, how can we become tall? For a self-centered person to become selfless seems just as impossible. And most poignantly, for a lustful, sexually impure person (a rapist? an abuser?) to become pure in heart seems totally impossible—so say our courts of law. (That's why we try to lock them up forever.)

And here comes Jesus telling us that "unless one is born again, he cannot see the kingdom of God" (John 3:3). To many people, that sounds like a death knell. "I am what I am, and there's no way I can become different! If only blue-eyed people can enter heaven, I'm sunk, for I have brown eyes!"

Sit down and read all the way through John 3. You'll be surprised how Jesus' explanation of the new birth is *very* Good News:

1. *Because of what He accomplished by His sacrifice, the Holy Spirit has become everyone's new "parents."* When He impregnated the Virgin Mary to bring Jesus to birth, He impregnated the human race with a divine seed of a new life to be formed within. He is constantly planting seeds of truth in human hearts, for Christ is "the true Light, which lighteth every man that cometh into the world" (John 1:9, KJV).

Encouraging people in the new birth is "just like a mother in childbirth. I feel the same kind of pain for you until Christ's nature is formed within you," says Paul (Galatians 4:19, GNB).

2. *The new birth is not you "born-ing" yourself anew (excuse me, we need that new verb!).* Jesus said, "The wind blows wherever it wishes. … It is like that with everyone who is born of the [Holy] Spirit" (John 3:8, GNB).

3. *Now, don't practice abortion on the new life that the Holy Spirit is constantly begetting within you. Stop resisting Him.* When you perceive what happened on the cross, you know that there is power there to transform the heart and the life. Paul put it this way:

"I am not ashamed of the gospel [Good News] of Christ, for it is the power of God to salvation for everyone who believes. … 'The just shall live by faith'" (Romans 1:16, 17). The same apostle told the Corinthians, "I determined not to know anything among you except Jesus Christ and Him crucified. … My preaching [was] not with persuasive words of human wisdom, but in demonstration of the Spirit and of power" (1 Corinthians 2:2-4). It's not impossible for us to understand just as clearly as the Corinthians understood!

What Turned the World Upside Down Was a Powerful Truth Buried in One Rather Obscure Word

The terrified enemies of the gospel confessed the impact of the apostles: "These who have turned the world upside down have come here too" (Acts 17:6).

The word that performed this mighty feat was one that was little used in the Greco-Roman world—the Greek term *agape*. It meant "love." But worlds different than our common idea of "love."

It came to carry a positive spiritual wallop that altered people's minds. It separated humanity into two camps, one for, and the other against the idea. Those who were for it were galvanized into dynamic followers of Jesus, ready to lose property, go to prison, or even die a tortured death.

On the other hand, those who reacted against it quickly became cruel, bloodthirsty persecutors of those who accepted the new idea of love. No one could hear the Good News about *agape* and stay neutral.

The mysterious explosive in this verbal "bomb" was a radically different idea of love that the world's philosophers or ethics teachers had never taught. It was a new invention that took friend and foe alike by surprise.

26

It wasn't that the ancients had no idea of love; they talked about it plenty. In fact, the Greeks had three or four words for it (our modern languages have only one). But the kind of love that is in the word *agape* mercilessly exposed all other ideas of love as either non-love or even anti-love.

Mankind suddenly realized that what they had been calling love was actually veneered selfishness. The human psyche was stripped naked by the new revelation. If you welcomed it, you got clothed with *agape* yourself. You were changed from the inside out.

If it made you angry, your robes of supposed piety being ripped off turned you into a raving enemy of the new faith. *Hence the persecutions.* And no one could turn the clock back, for *agape* was an idea for which the fullness of the time had come.

When John took his pen to write his famous equation, "God is love" (1 John 4:8), he had to choose between the several Greek words. The everyday one—*eros*—packed a powerful punch on its own. Something mysterious and powerful, *eros* was the source of all life. It swept like water from a broken dam over all obstacles of human will and wisdom, a tide of emotion common to all humanity. It was the source of the miracle of producing babies—deep mystery. If a mother loved her child, her love was *eros*—noble and pure. Likewise also the dependent love of children for their parents and the common love of friends for each other. And that mutual love of man and woman was something profound to be reckoned with.

Is God "Eros"? Asked the Ancient Pagans

Yes, answered their philosophers, including the great Plato, because *eros* is stronger than human will. It makes families and friends. And it dwells in everyone by nature. Therefore it must be the spark of divinity.

For the ancients, love was pretty much what "love" is for us today: the "sweet mystery of life," the elixir that makes an otherwise intolerable existence possible to endure. Plato hoped to transform the world by a kind of love that he considered "heaveny *eros*." Words derived from *eros* today have an exclusively sexual meaning, but Plato wanted the world to climb out of that swamp by a spiritually uplifting idea, noble and inspiring. It was based on climbing up higher, getting out of the mire of mere physical sensuality, being attracted to a greater good for the soul. Very spiritual.

But John could not bring himself to write that God is *eros*. He upset the thinkers of his day by saying, "God is *agape*." And between those two ideas there stretches a gulf wider than the east is from the west. There is no Good News and no power in *eros*, but both are in *agape*.

Two Ideas of Love in Contrast

How did *agape* differ so much from the common idea of love? How could the apostles' idea be such a threat to Plato's noble concept?

The answer is in several clear-cut contrasts:

1. ***Ordinary human love is dependent on the beauty or goodness of its object.*** We choose for friends those who are nice to us, who please us. We fall in love with our sexual opposite who is beautiful, happy, intelligent, and attractive, and turn away from one who is ugly, mean, ignorant, or offensive. In contrast, *agape* is not awakened by or dependent on beauty or goodness in its object. It stands alone, sovereign, independent. *Therefore it is free to love bad people, even enemies!* None of the ancients had ever dreamed of a love like this.

They had a story to illustrate their most sublime idea of it. Admetus, a noble, handsome young man with all the personal qualities of excellence fell sick with a disease that the oracle of the gods said would be fatal unless someone would die in his place. His friends went from one to another, "Would you be willing to die for Admetus?" "Sorry," they said, "we like him but we couldn't die for him." His parents were asked, and they said, "Oh, we love our son, but, sorry, we couldn't die for him." Finally his friends asked the beautiful girl who loved him, Alcestis. "Yes," she said, "because he is such a good man and because the world needs him so, I am willing to die for him!"

Crowed the philosophers: "*This* is love—someone willing to die for a good man!" But the apostles objected, that wasn't it at all. "One will hardly die for a righteous man—though perhaps for a good man one will dare even to die. But God shows his love [*agape*] for us in that while we were yet sinners [enemies, verse 10] Christ died for us" (Romans 5:7, 8, RSV). A message like that either captured your soul or made you raging angry.

2. ***Natural human love rests on a sense of need.*** It feels empty of itself, needs an object to enrich its own life. A husband loves his wife because he needs her, and a wife loves her husband for the same reason. Two friends love each other because they need each other. Each feels empty and alone without his counterpart.

Infinitely wealthy of itself, *agape* feels no need. The apostles said that the reason God loves us is not because He needs us, but because—well, He *is agape*. "You know the grace of our Lord Jesus Christ, that though He was rich, yet for your sakes He became poor, so that you through His poverty might become rich" (2 Corinthians 8:9). We are staggered by the idea of a love that "does not seek its own" (1 Corinthians 13:5). Even churches seem drawn to representing God's love as a seeking-its-own thing, a love inspired by a divine acquisitive instinct. God saw a hidden value in us, it is assumed; and He was simply making a good bargain when He "bought" us. This negates God's true love.

We come to resemble what we worship, so multitudes profess to worship such a "god" because they too are seeking a good bargain. Their religion is the soul of acquisitiveness—what they want to acquire is heaven and its rewards—and a self-centered motive is what keeps them going. When *agape* breaks through into this egocentric milieu, the reaction is pretty much what happened when it broke upon the world in apostolic times. Selfish hearts are transformed, and some "good" people get angry.

3. ***Natural human love rests on a sense of value.*** Many cultures still follow the bride-price system. The amount of the bride price is proportionate to the expense of education the girl's parents have invested in her. It used to be that a few cows sufficed for one who could barely scrawl her name; astronomical dowries were demanded for girls who had been to Oxford or Cambridge.

We also are the same in principle. We pigeonhole one another. Few treat the garbage man as courteously as they would the mayor or governor. If, like water seeking its own level, "you love those who love you, what reward have you? Do not even the tax collectors do the same? And if you greet your brethren only, what do you do more than others?" asks Jesus (Matthew 5:46, 47). "Men will praise you when you do well for yourself" (Psalm 49:18). We're all deeply selfish.

In contrast, *agape* is refreshingly different. Rather than being dependent on the value of its object, *it creates value in its object.*

Suppose I have a rough stone in my hand. I picked it up in a field. If I try to sell it, no one would give me even a nickel for it. This is not because the stone is inherently bad, but because it is so common it is worthless.

Now suppose as I hold this rough stone in my arms, that I could love it as a mother loves a baby. And suppose that my love could work like alchemy and transform it into a piece of solid gold. My fortune would be made.

This is an illustration of what *agape* does. Of ourselves we are worth nothing other than the dubious chemical value of our bodies' ingredients. But God's love transforms us into a value equivalent to that of His own Son: "I will make a mortal more rare than fine gold, a man more than the golden wedge of Ophir" (Isaiah 13:12).

Doubtless you have heard of a human derelict who has been transformed into a person of infinite worth. John Newton (1725-

1807) was such a one. A godless seafarer who dealt in the African slave trade, he became a drunken wretch who fell victim to the people he tried to enslave. At length *agape* touched his heart. He gave up his vile business and was transformed into an honored messenger of glad tidings. Millions remember him for his hymn that discloses the "fine gold" that he became:

> Amazing grace! how sweet the sound
> That saved a wretch like me!
> I once was lost, but now am found;
> Was blind, but now I see.
>
> 'Twas grace that taught my heart to fear
> And grace my fears relieved;
> How precious did that grace appear,
> The hour I first believed.

4. ***Natural human love thinks it must search for God***. All heathen religions are based on the idea of God being as elusive as a cure for cancer. People imagined that God is playing hide-and-seek and has withdrawn Himself from human beings. Only special ones are wise or clever enough to discover where He is hiding. Millions go on long journeys to Mecca, Rome, Jerusalem, or other shrines, searching for Him. The ancient Greeks outdid all of us in building magnificent marble temples in which they felt they must *seek* for God.

Again, *agape* proves to be the opposite. It is not humans seeking after God, but *God seeking after man*: "The Son of Man has come to seek and to save that which was lost" (Luke 19:10). The shepherd left his ninety-nine sheep that were safe and risked his life to find the one that was lost. The woman lit a candle and searched her house until she found the one lost coin. The Spirit of God searched for the heart of the prodigal son and brought him home. There is no story in all the Bible of a lost sheep that must go find his shepherd!

Paul was obsessed with this great idea: "The righteousness of faith speaks in this way, 'Do not say in your heart, "Who will ascend into heaven?"' (that is, to bring Christ down from above) or, '"Who will descend into the abyss?"' (that is, to bring Christ up from the dead). But what does it say? 'The word is near you, even in your mouth and in your heart' (that is, the word of faith which we preach)" (Romans 10:6-8).

That "word of faith" is as closely related to *agape* as a typeface is to its matrix. Faith is the response of a contrite human heart to this tremendous revelation of *agape*; and Paul's point is that this "word is *near* you." It proves that God has already sought you out where *you* have been hiding. The Good Shepherd is always on safari looking for us.

But doesn't the Bible say that it is up to us to "seek the Lord while He may be found" (Isaiah 55:6)? Yes; but the text goes on to emphasize God's *nearness*, not His *far-ness*. The Hebrew word for seek (*dharash*) means "inquire for," seek in the sense of choose. Isaiah continues, "Call upon Him while He is near," indicating that the Lord is already very close to us (see also Acts 17:27). The problem is we have not realized how close He is! Again, this idea blew people's minds.

5. *Our human love is always seeking to climb up higher*. Every first grader wants to enter the second grade; a child who is six says, "I will soon be seven." No job seeker wants *de*motion instead of *pro*motion. The state politician longs to get into the national game, and probably every national senator at some time dreams that he or she might make it to the White House.

Who has ever heard of a national president voluntarily resigning in order to become a village servant? Plato's idea of love could never imagine such a thing. Neither can we!

What amazed the ancient world was the sight of Someone higher than a president stepping down lower and lower, until He submitted to the torture-racked death of a criminal. In what is probably an outline of Paul's favorite message, we can trace in Philippians 2:5-8 (RSV) seven distinct downward steps that Christ took in telling us what *agape* is:

(1) *"Though He was in the form of God, [He] did not count equality with God a thing to be grasped"* (verse 6). When we get high up in politics, business, or even a church, it's our nature to worry about falling. "Uneasy lies the head that wears a crown," goes the old saying. But the Son of God abdicated His crown voluntarily, motivated by *agape*.

(2) *He "emptied Himself"* (verse 7), or "made Himself of no reputation" (NKJV). We humans will fight to the death for our honor or reputation. But daring deeds of valor aren't always the same as emptying oneself as Christ did, for one can give his "body to be burned" and yet lack *agape* (1 Corinthians 13:3). When Paul says Christ "emptied Himself," he was talking about a voluntary surrender for eternity of everything held dear, something quite impossible apart from *agape*.

(3) *He took "the form of a servant," literally, a slave* (verse 7). Can you imagine a more dismal life than always being forced to work without wages or thanks? Angels are said to be servants, "ministering spirits" sent to wait on us (Hebrews 1:14); if the Son of God had become

like one of them, that would have been a great condescension, for He was their Commander. But He stepped still lower:

(4) **He was "made in the likeness of men"** (verse 7, KJV)—"lower than the angels" (see Psalm 8:5). Not the sun-crowned, majestic splendor in which Genesis says Adam was created, but the degraded level of fallen man. It was the abysmal debasement common to the Greco-Roman world. No human being has ever fallen so low but that the Son of God has come far enough to reach him where he is. And once let that *agape* steal its way into our hearts, all lingering traces of any holier-than-thou spirit melt away before it, and we also find it possible to reach the hearts of others. We become the hearts and hands He uses to bless others.

(5) **"Being found in human form He humbled Himself"** (verse 8). In other words He was not born with the proverbial "silver spoon" in His mouth. Nor was He born in Caesar's or Herod's palace. His mother gave Him birth in a stinky cattle shed, forced to wrap her little one in rags and lay Him in a donkey's feed box. I have met only one person in Africa who said he was born in a cattle shed with the chickens and the goats! Christ became a toiling peasant. But this was not enough.

(6) **He "became obedient unto death"** (verse 8). This pregnant phrase means something different from the suicide's mad leap in the dark. No suicide is ever "*obedient* unto death. He is *dis*-obedient, he wants to escape reality. The kind of death Christ was "obedient" to was not an escape from responsibility. It was not like Socrates drinking his hemlock. It was the living, conscious condemnation of every cell of one's being before the demands of justice. The seventh step He took in condescension makes the degree of His self abasement clear:

(7) **"Even death on a cross"** (verse 8). In Jesus' day, a death on the cross was the most humiliating and hopeless possible. Not only was it one of the cruelest ever invented, but it was also one of the most shameful. One so condemned was suspended naked on a cross, and frequently the mob of onlookers watched with glee the dying man's agony. Death on such an instrument of execution carried a built-in horror all its own.

To Be Crucified Meant That Heaven Cursed You

The respected ancient writer Moses had declared that anyone who dies on a tree is "accursed by God" (Deuteronomy 21:23, RSV). And everybody believed it. If a condemned criminal was sentenced to be slain with a sword or even burned alive, he could still pray and trust that God would forgive him and look kindly on him. He could feel some support in his death.

But if the judge said, "You must die on a tree," all hope was gone. Everybody expected that God had turned His back on the wretch forever. This is why Paul says that Christ was "made a curse for us: for it is written, Cursed is every one that hangseth on a tree)" (Galatians 3:13, KJV). The kind of death Christ died was like that of the lost who must perish at last in hopeless despair—what Revelation calls "the second death" (2:11; 20:6, 14). Of course it was a million times worse for Christ to endure than it will be for them, because His sensitivity to the suffering was infinitely greater than for any of us.

Imagine a crucified man on a cross. Crowds come to jeer at him as today we flock to a ball game. Like an old, wrecked car that children throw rocks at, he is a human write-off, abandoned to be mocked and abused in horror unspeakable. You must not express or even feel pity or sympathy for him, for if you do you show that you disagree with God's judgment of him. You are on God's side if you throw rotten eggs or tomatoes at him and curse him. So people thought.

This was the death that Jesus became "obedient" to. In His despair He cried out, "My God, My God, why have You forsaken Me?" (Matthew 27:46). Be quiet and reverent as you think about it. You and I are the ones who would have had to go through that if He had not taken our place.

Incidentally, this idea of *agape* has been dying out among many professed followers of Christ because a pagan notion has subtly infiltrated our thinking—the doctrine of the natural immortality of the soul. That doctrine is really antichrist because it robs Him of His true love for the world. If there is no such thing as real death, then Christ did not really die. If He went to Paradise the day He died on the cross (as many mistakenly believe from reading a misplaced comma in Luke 23:43), then there was no true emptying of Himself, no true death on the cross, no dying the equivalent of the second death.

The doctrine of the natural immortality of the soul logically makes Christ's sacrifice a sham, a pretended stage play of enduring the wrath of God for sinners when in fact He was sustained throughout by the confidence of reward.

But when the darkness overtook Christ on Calvary, the light of His Father's face was, in fact, completely withdrawn. His cry, "Why have You forsaken Me?" was no actor's wail. Isaiah was right: "He poured out his soul unto death" (Isaiah 53:12)—the equivalent of "the second death."

Thus the pagan belief in man's natural immortality watered down the true meaning of *agape*. This began soon after the apostles' time, for Jesus warns the first of the seven symbolic churches of Revelation: "You have left your first love [*agape*]" (Revelation 2:4). When God's enemy saw the power packed in that idea of love, he first led the early church into apostasy on that essential point. It can be documented, step by step, the progressive abandonment of the idea of *agape* by the church fathers. Augustine worked out a synthesis of *agape* and self-centered love and called it *caritas*. It became the foundation of medieval Catholicism. Luther tried to restore *agape* to its right place, but sad to say, his followers returned to the doctrine of natural immortality, and again *agape* nearly died out. The world is now ripe for the resurgence of the biblical doctrine of *agape*.

Now We Sense the Gulf That Separates Human Love From *Agape*

Unless enriched with *agape*, our "love" *is really disguised selfishness*. Even parental love can be a mere "seeking our own."

Our present epidemic of marital infidelity is evidence enough of the self-centered aspect of sexual love. Often friends' love for each other is based on egocentric motivations. In contrast, *agape* "does not seek its own" and "never fails" (1 Corinthians 13:5, 8).

Having said all this, one additional contrast between human love and God's love remains: *Natural human love desires the reward of immortality; agape dares to relinquish it.* This was what overturned all the value systems of antiquity!

God has not written an encyclopedia for us explaining *agape*. Instead He sent His Son to die on a cross so we can see it. Its true meaning is that it is infinite, complete, and eternal. Christ went to the grave for us, not because He deserved it, but because we did. In those last few hours as He hung there in the darkness, He drained to its dregs the cup of human woe. The bright sunshine in which He had walked while on earth was gone. All thought of reward to come fled His mind. He could not see through to the other side of the dark and awful grave that gaped before Him. God *is agape*, and Christ is God, and there He is—dying the death we deserve. (The fact that the Father called Him back to life the third day in no way lessens the reality of His commitment on the cross in our behalf!)

Now we come to something disturbing. It's not enough for us to say, "Fine, glad He went through that; but you mean I must learn to love with *agape*? Impossible!"

The Good News declares that the love we think is impossible, God says is possible. We sinful, self-centered mortals *can* learn to love with *agape*, for John said: "Love [*agape*] is of God; and everyone who loves [with *agape*] is born of God and knows God. He who does not love [with *agape*] does not know God, for God is love [*agape*]" (1 John 4:7, 8). Moses is a prime example of one who learned it.

One day the Lord gave him a test. Israel had broken their covenant by worshiping a golden calf, and He proposed to Moses that He wipe them out with a divine "H-bomb" and start from scratch with a new people—Moses' descendants. Moses got the idea that Israel's sin was too great this time to be forgiven. The temptation to take the place of Abraham, Isaac, and Jacob as a new ethnic father was a very real one. He saw himself as facing a justifiably angry God who had had enough of Israel. It seemed vain for Moses to beg for Israel's forgiveness. So what did he do—accept the proffered honor, and let Israel go down the drain?

Moses was torn to his depths. He never cried so much in his life. Listen, as in broken sobs this mortal like ourselves tries to change God's mind:

"Oh, these people have sinned a great sin, and have made for themselves a god of gold! Yet now, if You will forgive their sin—..." Here Moses breaks down; he can't finish the sentence. He glimpses the horror of the loss of eternal life stretching before him if he shares Israel's fate. But he makes up his mind; he chooses to be lost with them: "...but if not, I pray, blot me out of Your book which You have written" (Exodus 32:31, 32).

Moses stood the test. I can imagine the Lord throwing His arms of love around His weeping servant—He had found a man after His own heart.

Paul had that same *agape* in his heart, for he also wished himself accursed from Christ for the sake of his lost people (see Romans 9:1-3). Everyone who sees the cross as it truly is, and believes, finds the miracle of *agape* reproduced in his own heart. He discovers for himself how true it is that "the gospel [Good News] of Christ ... is the power of God to salvation for everyone who believes" (Romans 1:16). His attention is lifted away from himself, in whom there is no salvation, to the real source of power.

Can you think how anything could be better news than *agape*? Look at it; "*behold*, what manner of love the Father hath bestowed upon us" (1 John 3:1, KJV). Could anything be easier than to look?

Your Personal Notes

That was the true Light which gives light to every man coming into the world. He was in the world, and the world was made through Him, and the world did not know Him (John 1:9, 10).

4

The Only Antidote to Terror: Pulling Up the Root of Fear

(What makes terror fearful is what agape destroys)

E ven animals have a built-in fear. From our earliest conscious moment, this nameless dread of the unknown oppresses all of us. All through life, even to our dying moments, we live constantly on its threshold. Happy and secure one moment, we can be in terror the next, and down come our "Trade Towers."

Fear with its root of anxiety is the substratum of human existence. Too deep for us to understand, it can make us sick, gnawing at the vitals of the soul until even one's physical organs weaken and become susceptible to disease. Years may go by before we can see or feel its ravages, but at last the weakened organs break down, and doctors must go to work to try to repair the damage that fear has caused.

This universal fact of human nature is recognized in one of the most joyful statements of Good News to be found. *Christ delivers us from the Bad News of fear*:

> "Since the children have flesh and blood, He too shared in their humanity so that by His death He might destroy him who holds the power of death—that is, the devil—and free those who all their lives were held in slavery by their fear of death" (Hebrews 2:14, 15, NIV; that word "destroy" in the original means "to paralyze").

So long as we know that fear of death, just so long are we "held in slavery." Generally speaking, the more one enjoys life and the healthier he or she is in mind and body, the greater his abhorrence of death.

Death is not simply like going to sleep. Sleep is welcome rest, but death is terrifying. It is the conscious, devastating dissolution of all that makes the individual a person. This means that every threat to our uniqueness or worth as a person has overtones of that ultimate threat, "fear of death," from which Christ came to deliver us.

Anything that diminishes our personhood is an aspect of that "fear of death" that humans know "all their lives." This constant sense of insecurity that plagues all humans in one form or another is what the book of Hebrews is talking about.

Don't let anyone kid you into thinking you don't have this problem. If you're human, you will come to terms with it. Even kings and presidents know it. When a United States president was faced with the prospect of losing the presidency in disgrace, he came almost emotionally unglued. So would any intelligent person in similar circumstances, unless, of course, he has fully appropriated the "Good News" we are talking about. Whether one is a teenager or in his 90s, the diminishing of one's sense of self-worth is an annihilating experience, and all degrees of it are an approach to that ultimate diminishment—death.

How *Agape* Frees Us From the Slavery of Fear

Since the sacrifice of Christ perfectly demonstrates *agape*, it is the perfect remedy for fear. "There is no fear in love [*agape*]; but perfect love casteth out fear: because fear hath torment. He that feareth is not made perfect in love [*agape*]" (1 John 4:18, KJV). The reason this is true is that as *agape* confronts *ultimate* fear and vanquishes it, in the process it overcomes all lesser fears.

Three realities underscore this truth:

1. *When He became man, Christ became our personal representative or subsitute, more so than any lawyer represents a client in a criminal court case.* The Bible says that because of Adam's sin we all die (see 1 Corinthians 15:22; Romans 5:12). Thus we inherited from Adam not only death but the slavery to the fear of death. The whole human race was "in Adam."

This is evident from the fact that without Adam we wouldn't exist. But the Good News immediately says, "Even so in Christ all shall be made alive" (1 Corinthians 15:22). Christ's victory over death and the fear of death therefore automatically becomes *our* victory by virtue of this corporate oneness with Him. He has effected that for all of us. (Remember, God is no respecter of persons—all share in these benefits unless they choose not to.)

So real is this experienced oneness with Christ that Paul can say, "*I* have been crucified *with* Christ; it is no longer I who live, but Christ lives in me; and the life which I now live in the flesh I live by faith in the Son of God, who loved me and gave Himself for me" (Galatians 2:20). Faith is the glue that cements us to Christ's experience, as it were. Something more intimate than sympathy or even empathy unites us to Him, and His death to sin and fear becomes our death to sin and fear.

This oneness-with-Him is also seen in Paul's expression, "If One died for all, then all died" (2 Corinthians 5:14). All died *with* Him, and faith is simply experiencing His death and victory over our enemy, living our way through it. Faith is what enables us to feel how Jesus felt when He went through that cross experience. Faith actually enters into His love, into His experience, and this is how He expels fear from our hearts. What Christ went through, we go through, all "by faith."

The Bible does not teach that Christ's substitution for us leaves us alone, so we are excused from understanding and appreciating what He went through. He asked His drowsy disciples to "watch with Me one hour" and was disappointed that they had so little interest that they were children in that most fateful hour of earth's history, the climax of their Master's agony (see Matthew 26:40). The more closely we can identify with Him in that "hour" when He conquered fear, the more complete will be our release from fear. Every person truly crucified with Christ (through faith) learns to scorn fear.

Since Satan is the author of fear and employs terror as one of his most effective tools, it is obvious that he wants to hide from us this discovery of Christ's cross. It was there that Satan was "cast down" (Revelation 12:10). One of his prime lies is to tell us it's impossible for us to understand what happened when Christ died for us, anymore than we can understand all the commercial intricacies of our insurance company's organization. "Just trust it," that's all, "and turn your attention elsewhere," is what we think is the extent of our "Christian experience." Just "trust Him," that's all; and be content to remain an infant in understanding.

But That Grieves Him Immensely

Satan wants us to remain infants in understanding what it means. It's true that as finite humans we can never *fully* appreciate that sacrifice, but to be content not to grow in our appreciation of it is a cop-out equivalent to despising it. Our intelligent identification with Christ in His death makes possible our sharing in His conquest of fear and death.

Not only does Christ hunger for our closer fellowship with Him, He is disappointed when we don't seek it. How would you feel if you had risked your life to save a loved one, and then he flippantly thanks you with the superficial appreciation appropriate for picking up a nickel he had dropped? One of the reasons many are to a large extent still in slavery to fear is that they understand and appreciate all too little what it cost Him to redeem us.

2. *Our personal faith in Christ makes possible our sharing with Him His victory over fear.* We all know how we tend to identify with an actor in a movie or a drama. Many go so far in identifying that they weep unashamedly in sympathy with the actor or actress. There is nothing redemptive in sharing such experiences vicariously, but when *"we see Jesus"* in His sacrificial agonies for us, *there is redemption.* Identification with Him brings healing to the soul, because He truly identified with us and that effects for us an identification with Him. The agenda for Christ's battle to conquer fear and death is outlined as follows:

> "We see Jesus, who was made a little lower than the angels, for the suffering of death crowned with glory and honor, that He, by the grace of God, might taste death for everyone. For it was fitting for Him, for whom are all things and by whom are all things, in bringing many sons to glory, to make the author of their salvation perfect through sufferings. For both He who sanctifies and those who are being sanctified are all of one, for which reason He is not ashamed to call them brethren. ... Inasmuch then as the children have partaken of flesh and blood, He Himself likewise shared in the same, that through death He might destroy him who had the power of death, that is, the devil, and release those who through fear of death were all their lifetime subject to bondage" (Hebrews 2:9-11, 14, 15).

If we were to "taste" our own real death ourselves, the poison of it would do us in forever, for there is no hope of a resurrection after "the second death" (see Revelation 2:11; 20:14). Such a final death involves a horror of utter self-condemnation totally and eternally destructive to human personality. Since human beings are finite creatures, in no way can they endure total destruction for an infinite duration. To hold such a view is a contradiction of terms. It is the consciousness of being condemned in judgment and shut out from light and life forever that is the real pain of "the second death."

Jesus "tasted" this death "for everyone" as He hung on the cross in the darkness. Himself the Blessed One, He was made "a curse for us (for it is written, 'Cursed is everyone who hangs on a tree')" (Galatians 3:13). The feeling of being forsaken by His Father was drinking a bitter cup of sorrow unsweetened by the tiniest taste of hope.

Although Jesus feared death (see Hebrews 5:7), it is not right to say that He *yielded* to this fear. He *faced* the fear of eternal separation from God, and "for everyone" He felt the total unspeakable horror of its essence. Yet He conquered it totally.

The True Dimension of Christ's Love for Us

With the deepest reverence, we might say that Christ figuratively went to hell, and then came back. The apostle Peter at Pentecost seems to have recognized that this was the true nature of His sacrifice: "God raised Him from the dead, freeing Him from the agony of death, because it was impossible for death to keep its hold on Him" (Acts 2:24, NIV). The *King James Version* renders as follows Peter's quotation from Psalm 16:10: "Thou wilt not leave my soul in hell; neither wilt Thou suffer Thine Holy One to see corruption." ("hell" [Hebrew: *sheol*] here means an eternal grave.) When Christ "poured out His soul unto death" (Isaiah 53:12), He felt that His Father had "forsaken" Him forever.

None of us can duplicate Christ's sacrifice, for that would be impossible. He was the infinite Son of God, and we are mere creatures whose sacrifice (if we could make it) would be meaningless. We can never be co-saviors of ourselves. But we can *appreciate* His sacrifice for us.

This burns out of our souls our petty little self-centered motivations. Amazed and awed by the *agape* that led Jesus to His cross, we "pour contempt" on our selfish desires to avoid the punishment of eternal death and win Paradise because of its rewards. Suddenly an entirely new motivation grips our souls—the passion to honor and glorify the One who redeemed us at such infinite cost. It's saying "Thank You for saving our souls!" In that gratitude, selfish motivations are transcended.

As surely as day follows night, this new motivation expels the root of fear. When faith identifies with Christ, one never again feels alone and bereft, for we have participated by faith in Christ's death-grapple with the enemy in His awful hours on Calvary. Christ has built the bridge that spans the chasm of eternal death; now we simply cross over it "in Him."

How *Agape* Alone Can Meet the Final Test

Bible prophecy tells us that fear and terror will constitute the final test of "the mark of the beast." So exquisite will be Satan's perfected method of temptation that he will sweep into his ranks all who then remain susceptible to terror imposed by the sinful slavery of fear.

> "He causes all, both small and great, rich and poor, free and slave, to receive a mark on their right hand or on their foreheads, and that no one may buy or sell except one who has the mark or the name of the beast, or the number of his name" (Revelation 13:16, 17).

Modern society is uprooted from its attachment to the land and agriculture, huddled in vulnerable megalopolises, utterly dependent for survival on economic integration, with peoples' minds conditioned by clever mass media presentations that major in horror movies and political herding. All this will combine to make death become the most terror-inducing threat that man has ever known.

And we can be sure that the author of "the mark of the beast" will also concoct a terror-inspiring spiritual fear through fiendish counterfeits of a false christ and a false holy spirit. Included in that final test will be his manufactured threat of God's eternal condemnation of all who dare to stand up for truth. If we are still subject to fear, down we will go!

This threat of starvation and of economic and social ostracism will terrify multitudes who have never learned *agape* by kneeling with Jesus in His Gethsemane.

But there will be a "remnant" who face this terror-inducing threat with holy calmness. They are described first of all as those "whose names have … been written in the Book of Life of the Lamb slain from the foundation of the world" (Revelation 13:8). *Fellowship with Christ in His capacity as the crucified Lamb is the secret of their fearlessness.* They are also identified as "those who keep the commandments of God" (Revelation 14:12). True keeping of the commandments is the experience of *agape*, for only "love [*agape*] is the fulfillment of the law" (Romans 13:10).

3. *John adds another insight as to how love conquers fear.* "Love [*agape*] has been perfected among us in this: that we may have boldness in the day of judgment; because as He is, so are we in this world" (1 John 4:17). Without such *agape*, it is inevitable that one must cringe in terror when confronted with this ultimate judgment. But with *agape*, he walks fearlessly into God's presence, past all the holy angels, utterly

unashamed and unafraid. Those who identify with Christ are "Marines" who have fought side by side in the fiercest, most dangerous battles with the enemy of our souls, unfazed by peril. Our faith-participation "with Christ" in His atonement has uprooted fear from our souls, because the self-centered motivation is uprooted. Thus there is nothing left in the soul that the presence of judgment can burn in condemnation.

"God forbid that I should boast except in the cross of our Lord Jesus Christ, by whom the world has been crucified to me, and I to the world" (Galatians 6:14). The Good News of that cross will be a never-ending joy.

Your Personal Notes

For the love of Christ compels us, because we judge thus: that if One died for all, then all died; and He died for all, that those who live should live no longer for themselves, but for Him who died for them and rose again (2 Corinthians 5:14, 15).

5

God Keeps on Trying to Save Us

(Nobody else is so persistent!)

I f God tries to save us and then gives up when He sees how difficult we are, that is Bad News. If He has made the path to heaven difficult and the path to perdition easy, that is also Bad News.

Deep Down, How Do You Feel About God?

One way to find out would be to ask yourself whether this statement is true or false: "It's easy to be lost and hard to be saved." If you answer "True," it is likely that your basic idea of God is uncomfortably like that of the one-talent man who dug a hole and buried His wealth in the ground. When the Lord finally confronted him, he retorted, "'Master, I knew you to be a hard man, reaping where you did not sow, and gathering where you did not winnow; so I was afraid'" (Matthew 25:24, 25, RSV).

Many people today fear God and view Him as a pretty "hard man," who lets it be difficult for us to be saved, but easy for us to be lost. And if that's true, then God sits by unconcerned while the vast majority of earth's inhabitants are allowed to slide into eternal lostness, unwarned. He lets the path to hell be a superhighway down which you coast effortlessly into eternal ruin.

And further, if this common idea is true, then He hides the way to heaven so cleverly with every conceivable obstacle fiendishly built into it to discourage as many people as possible. And God stands back in the shadows, content to watch the masses slide down this slippery path to perdition, while only a mere handful have what it takes to thread their way through that maze and make it to heaven. And this is supposed to be "Good News"?

The natural human heart, apart from a distinct miracle, is "enmity with God" (Romans 8:7, NEB). Anybody who thinks he never has had this problem is naive, for "we all once lived in the passions of our flesh, following the desires of body and mind, and so we were by nature children of wrath, like the rest of mankind" (Ephesians 2:3, RSV). A good way to start getting this buried "wrath" out of our inmost soul is to discover the truth: *it is indeed hard to be lost, and easy to be saved if one understands and believes how good the Good News is.* God is a much more likable character than we have been prone to think, and His Good News is a lot better than we have thought.

There ought not to be any question about something if Jesus says it plainly. Yet multitudes who say they believe the Bible balk at one of His clearest utterances: "Come to Me, all you who labor and are heavy laden, and I will give you rest. … For My yoke is easy and My burden is light" (Matthew 11:28-30). Human nature seems intent on believing that His yoke is hard. Many feel that being a true Christian is a fiendishly difficult undertaking, a heroic achievement that only a few can ever hope to realize.

Naturally Such an Idea Discourages Multitudes Who Want to Follow Jesus

Let's look also at the apostle Paul's report of a personal conversation with God on his way to Damascus. Paul, then known as Saul, was truly hell-bent, fuming with rage against the followers of Jesus, determined to fight against this faith to the last ounce of his strength. He had money, official influence, public opinion, and ecclesiastical sanction on his side. Did he find this path "easy"?

Outwardly, perhaps. But wait. We might assume that he was on a toboggan ride to hell. But the same Jesus, who tells us that His "yoke is easy," told Saul: *the way you're going is actually "hard."*

This is how Paul described his experience:

> "I was travelling to Damascus with authority and commission from the chief priests; and as I was on my way, Your Majesty [King Agrippa], in the middle of the day I saw a light from the sky, more brilliant than the sun, shining all around me. … then I heard a voice saying to me in the Jewish language, 'Saul, Saul, why do you persecute me? It is hard for you, this kicking against the goad. … I am Jesus, whom you are persecuting'" (Acts 26:12-15, NEB).

God's Persevering Love

The fact is that God truly loved Saul. The poor man was hell-bent, but the obstacles were placed in the supposed superhighway to hell, not the path to heaven! Sinner Saul was meeting up with all kinds of inner difficulties that made his way "hard." The Holy Spirit loved him so much that He constantly pressed into his soul the conviction of sin. Day and night Saul felt the "goad": What you're doing is wrong, Saul. Stop! Turn around! Danger ahead!

No way did the Holy Spirit allow Saul to slide unhindered down a greased runway to perdition. In order for him to go on in his mad campaign against Christ, Saul would have had to repress and stultify all these convictions and promptings of the Holy Spirit. The Lord loved Saul so much that He made it "hard" for him to destroy himself.

When Saul became the apostle Paul, he never forgot the lesson. He had discovered "Good News." And the Lord loves us no less than He loved this wayward man of old.

Christ is the "true Light which gives light to every man who comes into the world" (John 1:9). The Holy Spirit does not restrict this good work to only a handful of favorite people, but "He will convict the world of sin" (John 16:8). "God ... desires all men to be saved" (1 Timothy 2:3, 4, RSV). *Don't go on frustrating Him!*

Something Often Misread

As an example of Paul's irrepressible "Good News," consider one of his passages that is usually misconstrued to say the opposite of what he intended: "The desires of the flesh are against the Spirit, and the desires of the Spirit are against the flesh; for these are opposed to each other, to prevent you from doing what you would" (Galatians 5:17, RSV).

There are two ways to understand this: (1) The evil that the flesh prompts us to do is so strong that even the Holy Spirit is powerless to help us, and we simply cannot do the (good) things that we "would." Or (2), the good that the Holy Spirit prompts the believer to do becomes such a powerful motivation that the flesh loses its tyrannical control over him, and the Holy Spirit prevents the believer in Christ "from doing" the evil things that he "would" otherwise be programmed to do.

Explanation (1) is Bad News. The idea is that as long as you have "flesh" in which to live, you are doomed to continual defeat. This is what many feel forced to believe. Their experience constantly seems to reinforce this idea; for they find the "flesh" all-powerful. Illicit love, sensuality, cigarette addiction, alcoholism, drugs, or materialism beat back the Spirit; and temptation makes them cave in repeatedly. Surely the Lord's heart goes out to them. He knows how many times they have stained their pillows with tears as they review their day's failures.

Explanation (2) emerges as the best Good News one could imagine. The Holy Spirit is actually doing the work; He works "against the flesh." Whereas we may have thought that obstacles impeded our path *to heaven*, making it as difficult as possible, the reality is *that He sets up obstacles in our way to perdition.* He is stronger than the "flesh." Every moment of every day, He makes His influence apparent "against the flesh," against these promptings of our sinful natures, and *with our consent* completely defeats them all. He spends as much time with each person in this constant striving against evil as if that person were the only one on earth.

Which of the Two Explanations Is the Correct One?

When allowed to speak in context, the Bible unhesitatingly says, the Good News one; for it alone is in harmony with Jesus' words about His yoke being "easy." It is because He knows that the mighty Holy Spirit does the lifting of the heavy weight that He assures us, "My burden is light."

But don't be fooled into thinking that when you are converted, your sinful nature will never again prompt you to do evil things. We don't have "holy flesh" so long as we're in this sinful world. A truly converted person is still temptable, maybe even more so than before. Jesus Himself was "one who in every respect has been tempted as we are" (Hebrews 4:15, RSV). Is anybody better than He was?

The one who follows Christ has the same sinful flesh he always had, but he is no longer a slave to "*gratify* the desires of the flesh" (Galatians 5:16, RSV). He is now "led by the Spirit" (verse 18, RSV) into a new "freedom" (verse 1, RSV).

We have Someone on our side who is more than a Savior in name only: "For God has done what the law, weakened by the flesh, could not do: sending His own Son in the likeness of sinful flesh and for sin, He condemned sin in the flesh, in order that the just requirement of the law might be fulfilled in us, who walk not according to the flesh but according to the Spirit" (Romans 8:3, 4, RSV).

Someone May Ask, "How Come I Never Knew This Before?"

"I have wasted years while laboring under a misapprehension!" An enemy has masterminded a scheme to obscure the pure, true gospel and has twisted it into Bad News.

If you are beginning ever so slightly to see God in a different light as One who is on your side as you never imagined He is, be glad for the revelation.

Almost everybody these days has the feeling TV is stronger than the prayer meeting—the lure of the world has more appeal than the service of God. Like a weak distant signal jammed by a powerful radio station nearby, the Holy Spirit seems barely able to come through, compared with the appeal of the world. But Paul says, No: "Where sin abounded, grace abounded much more, so that as sin reigned in death, even so grace might reign through righteousness to eternal life through Jesus Christ our Lord" (Romans 5:20, 21). Heaven's signal is stronger!

Before we understood the gospel, Paul says, "sin reigned" like a king, beating back the power of grace like Saul kicking against the "goad." But when we understand the gospel, grace reigns like a king and beats back the power of sin. This has to be true, because if there is not more power in grace than there is in temptation, John would be wrong when he says, "This is the victory that has overcome the world—our faith" (1 John 5:4). That would mean that the gospel could not be Good News.

Remember, the battle is never an even one: it's not 50/50. Grace abounds "*much more*." It is literally true that "if anyone is in Christ, he is a new creation; old things have passed away; behold, all things have become new" (2 Corinthians 5:17). You have a new Father, so that the power working within you for good is as much stronger than our tendencies to evil, as our heavenly Father is greater than our earthly parents.

A Fabulous Discovery

The wonderful Bible truth is that *God takes the initiative in saving us.* He is not, as many conceive of Him, standing back, His divine arms folded in disinterested unconcern while we wallow in our misery. He is not saying, "Well, I did My part long ago; it's up to you now. You must take the initiative. If you want to be saved, come and work hard at it. If it seems hard to you, you just don't have what it takes to get to heaven."

No. A thousand times No! But many feel that way about God. And some shy and timid ones think God has plenty of good people ready to take my place—He doesn't need *me*, and I'm not really sure He even wants me.

In contrast, Paul helps us see the divine initiative at work for us: "Do you despise the riches of His goodness, forbearance, and longsuffering, not knowing that the goodness of God leads you to repentance?" (Romans 2:4).

The *Good News Bible* says He "is trying to lead you to repent." The goodness of God is actually taking you by the hand and leading you toward repentance as surely as a fireman tries to lead a victim out of the smoke and haze of a burning building. If you don't stubbornly resist, you will be led all the way to heaven. Astounding as it may seem, that's the message.

Sometimes we pray agonizingly for some wayward loved one, assuming we have to beg the Lord to wake up and please do something. The idea is that He is divinely indifferent until we touch His pity somehow. But the goodness of God is already working, leading your loved one to repentance. The trouble is that we often thwart what He is trying to do because we haven't understood that goodness, mercy, and forbearance of the Lord in their true dimensions. We're horrified to realize it, but we pile stumbling blocks in our loved one's way to heaven. We don't realize how the selfishness and inconsistencies they see in us block their access to God, or shadow their concepts of His character.

And it is true, not everybody repents. Why? Some "despise" this goodness of God. Stubborn, they break away from that leading. Let's grasp this tremendous insight! The sinner may resist this love, he may refuse to be drawn to Christ; but if he does not resist he will be drawn to Jesus. A knowledge of the plan of salvation will lead him to the foot of the cross in repentance for his sins.

This Is a Revolutionary Idea to Many People

They have supposed that they must take the initiative and *do* something first if they want to be saved. To them this Good News idea seems putting the cart before the horse—if we stop resisting, we will be saved! But however revolutionary it sounds, this is the "Good News" of the gospel, for it presupposes the active, persistent love of God. It leaps at you in beautiful thoughts like this one from Paul:

> "This is what I mean: so long as the heir is a minor, he is no better off than a slave, even though the whole estate is his; he is under guardians and trustees until the date fixed by his father. And so it was with us. During our minority we were slaves to the elementary ideas belonging to this world [margin], but when the term was completed, God sent His own Son, born of a woman, born under the law, to purchase freedom for the subjects of the law, in order that we might attain the status of sons" (Galatians 4:1-5, NEB).

This mind-boggling idea discloses the reality of God's true character of love. He counts all humans as potential heirs of His "estate," but "before this faith came" to us individually in our experience, we are like the millionaire estate owner's barefoot child who is bossed about by common slaves. We come of age when we grasp the Good News truth by faith. Until then, we remain "prisoners" and the law is our "schoolmaster," tutor who maneuvers us to the Savior (Galatians 3:24; KJV, Greek; a slave who conducted children to school and whipped them if they got off the path). The law can't save; but it can drive us to the Savior who can!

And what we don't learn easily by faith, by His grace, we learn a harder way by discipline. The Savior doesn't give up! All this infinite, loving care is lavished upon us individually in order to lead us to Christ, that we might "be justified by faith"!

God Has a Bigger Circle

It's so easy for us naive humans to conceive of the Lord as drawing a circle that shuts out bad people. But He draws a bigger circle to include them—at least until they shut Him out by never-ending resistance.

The Lord looks upon lost people not as wolves to be shot down as soon as possible, but as sheep who have wandered away—as potential heirs to His estate. His grace persists in seeking some way to intrude. What a pity that so many church people don't yet understand this concept and consequently treat "unsaved" people as if they were wolves! The church has hardly begun to love as God loves! That idea of *agape* is slow to grasp, it seems.

Being "justified by faith" is something that nearly staggers one's mind just to realize how wonderful it is. It makes you want to get up on the housetop and shout the news to everybody. Christ's death on the cross is for every sinner—it's a sacrifice for his or her salvation. God has no chip on His shoulder against anyone. And this "gift" is "out of all proportion" to sin, which is "*vastly exceeded* by the grace of God" (Romans 5:15, NEB). Thus there is no reason why "everyone" should not be saved except that they refuse Christ's grace and spurn the "gift" of salvation.

In his same letter Paul goes a step further and says that "God has dealt to each one a measure of faith" (Romans 12:3). So, (a) God has brought justification for "everyone" by the sacrifice of His Son, and (b) He has given "each one a measure of faith" to appropriate that justification. Would that everyone said Yes and *exercised* the faith already given him!

51

What More Could God Do?

It all adds up to the conclusion that, if anyone is lost at last, it will be because of his or her own persistent rejection of what God has already done to save him. And if anyone is saved, it will be because he stopped resisting God's initiative in saving him!

C. S. Lewis expresses this idea in his book, *The Great Divorce*. He puts it as a parable, imagining the Holy City to be a mere bus ride away from hell, and all in hell who wish to move there are welcome. But when they come to visit, they can't stand the place. Even the blades of grass cut their feet like knives! They want to board the bus back to hell as soon as possible. The lost shut themselves out of heaven. It's not by any arbitrary decree of God, but by their own chosen inability to be happy there, that they end up outside the city.

In the final analysis, therefore, whether one is saved or lost depends on his *choice*, the response he chooses to give to what God *has already done* for him, not what God *might do* for him if he (the sinner) takes the initiative.

In the light of the love of God revealed at the cross, even the choice to be saved becomes "easy." Granted, if we eclipse the cross of Christ, we must admit that it becomes terribly hard to follow Christ. In fact, impossible. The springs of motivation dry up, and temptation to evil becomes overpowering in its appeal. The Savior becomes "a root out of dry ground," and His gospel contains "no beauty that we should desire Him" (Isaiah 53:2). But if we see the unadulterated grace of Christ, even that choice to bear the cross with Him becomes easy. The love of Christ constrains the one who appreciates what He has done and strengthens him to choose to respond.

What Part Do We Have to Do?

Someone may ask, Didn't Jesus say, "Strive to enter through the narrow gate"? (Luke 13:24). Aren't we to be "striving against sin"? (Hebrews 12:4). Isn't there hard work for us to do?

Yes, there are indeed endless conflicts with temptation. We are soldiers in a battle. But the point is that we never have to fight alone. We are joined in a yoke with Christ—He does the pulling and our job is to cooperate with Him, to stop resisting. "*Let* this mind be in you which was also in Christ Jesus" (Philippians 2:5). The part we have to do is tremendously important, for God will not force a person to be saved against his or her will. The Bible says it over and over:

"*Let* this mind be in you which was also in Christ Jesus" (Philippians 2:5). "*Let* the peace of God rule in your hearts, to which also you were called in one body, … *Let* the word of Christ dwell in you richly in all wisdom" (Colossians 3:15, 16). That's our part! It's as though God takes you by the hand and tugs, saying, "Let's go … to heaven!" Don't resist Him, don't squirm away.

It's a joy for a pupil to have a good teacher who makes the learning process easy. Our Savior is also our Teacher who specializes in teaching us how to say one important word:

> "The grace of God that brings salvation has appeared to all men. It teaches us to say 'No' to ungodliness and worldly passions, and to live self-controlled, upright and godly lives in this present age, while we wait for the blessed hope—the glorious appearing of our great God and Savior, Jesus Christ, who gave Himself for us to redeem us from all wickedness and to purify for Himself a people that are His very own, eager to do what is good" (Titus 2:11-14, NIV).

That word "No" may seem to be the hardest word you have ever pronounced, but even here God does not abandon you to stumble along on your own until you say it right. "The grace of God" will *teach* you how to say it! Can you imagine better news than that?

Note that the secret you have to learn is to remember how Christ "gave Himself for us to redeem us." We are never farther away than a hair's breadth from that cross!

And note also that it is *He* who does the "purifying" of a people "for Himself … , eager to do what is good" (Titus 2:14, NIV). "It is God who works in you both to will and to do for His good pleasure" (Philippians 2:13). *Let* Him do it!

Our own individual effort is, of course, useless apart from the grace of Christ, but if we don't lose sight of Him being with us, our part is always easy.

Was His Part "Easy" for Him in Gethsemane and on His Cross?

No, a thousand times, No! His stern battle with self in the garden and on the cross was so severe that He sweat drops of blood; even His very heart was ruptured in His final agony. Does that mean that He was telling us a lie when He said, "My burden is light"?

No. The burden He speaks of in Matthew 11:30 is the burden that *we carry*; His was infinitely heavy. The faith that works through love (see Galatians 5:6) makes our burden light for us to carry, for we appreciate the heaviness it was to Him.

The only difficult thing in following Him, therefore, is the choice to surrender self to be "crucified with Christ" (Galatians 2:20). However, we are never called to be crucified alone—only *with Him*. It is infinitely easier for us to be crucified with Christ than it was for Him to be crucified alone for us.

Even if this still seems hard, don't ever forget that it remains much harder to go on fighting against love like that and beating off the persistent leading of the Holy Spirit in order to be lost.

6

You Are Predestined
To Be Saved!

(Really? The News gets better and better!)

There are thoughtful people who actually believe that God predestines some to be saved and predestines some to be lost, irrespective of their real wishes.

This is discouraging to those who find it hard to believe that God would choose *them* to be among the fortunate few. One who thinks he has been numbered among the unlucky ones will naturally do one of two things: (1) live in despair, or (2) abandon himself to a life of sin.

If such a doctrine of "predestination" were true, one can hardly imagine any Bad News that could be worse than to receive God's irrevocable rejection slip.

And to make matters worse, those who have believed in such predestination usually believe that the unlucky lost will roast and sizzle consciously in terrible flames for all eternity, writhing and screaming in endless horror, while the vengeful God who sent them there looks on nodding His head in approval.

The Bible Paints an Infinitely
Better Picture of God Than That

There is a Bible teaching of predestination, but when you examine it you find that it is quite different from the one many have assumed it to be. *God has predestined everyone to be saved.* And the only way anyone can be lost is to veto the vote that God has already given in his favor; in other words, they must undo the salvation that the Lord has already wrought out for him.

Let us look at some samples of Bible teaching on this matter:

1. *"God our Savior" wants "all men to be saved and to come to the knowledge of the truth"* (1 Timothy 2:3, 4). But He does more than sit idly by, "wanting" all to be saved. He does something to bring it about.

2. *Jesus said that by His cross He would reach out and touch "all men."* "'I, when I am lifted up from the earth, will draw all men to myself.' He said this to show the kind of death He was going to die" (John 12:32, 33, NIV). *He is doing something!*

3. *He is "the true Light which gives light to every man who comes into the world"* (John 1:9). His drawing or pulling is gentle, for He will force no one against his will; but He is firm and persistent. There is no morally responsible human being anywhere in the world who can either read or hear these words who has not been enlightened somehow by that Light, or felt His drawing power in some way.

4. *Thus "the God and Father of our Lord Jesus Christ ... chose us in Him before the creation of the world to be holy and blameless in His sight.* In love He predestined us to be adopted as His sons through Jesus Christ, in accordance with His pleasure and will" (Ephesians 1:4, NIV)

5. *"In Him we were also chosen, having been predestined according to the plan of Him who works out everything in conformity with the purpose of His will"* (Ephesians 1:11, NIV). Paul gives no hint that anyone is excluded or predestined to be lost. He means all in the human race are chosen. Your job is to welcome the Good News.

6. *God sees things before they happen, and He knows people before they are born.* When Jeremiah came to understand how God loved him, the Lord told him:

> Before I formed you in the womb I knew you,
> before you were born I set you apart;
> I appointed you as a prophet.
> —Jeremiah 1:5, NIV

You may not be called to be a prophet, but He has chosen you for a career of happiness now and forever.

7. *In the same way, the Lord has "appointed" every person to be saved*, and His Holy Spirit is working to lead "all men ... to a knowledge of the truth" (1 Timothy 2:4, NIV). *This does not mean that everyone will at last be saved.* Sad to say, many will be lost, but it will not be the fault of God, nor the result of His rejecting them. *It will be their rejecting Him.*

8. *The Good News is set forth powerfully in these words*: "We know that in all things God works for the good of those who love Him, who have been called according to His purpose. For those God foreknew He also predestined to be conformed to the likeness of His Son. ... And those He predestined, He also called; those He called, He also justified; those He justified, He also glorified. ... If God is for us, who can be against us? He who did not spare His own Son, but gave Him up for us all—how will He not also, along with Him, graciously give us all things? ... I am convinced that neither death nor life, ... neither height nor depth, nor anything else in all creation, will be able to separate us from the love [*agape*] of God that is in Christ Jesus our Lord" (Romans 8:28-39, NIV).

Is There a Hidden Catch Here, Some "Fine Print" That Excludes Some People From This Good News?

No. Paul simply assumes that his readers join him in responding to this wonderful love (*agape*) of God. If we don't resist, we are included in the family. The happy thing is that those who respond are "predestined" to be changed into absolutely beautiful people "conformed to the likeness of His Son!" The predestination is progressive.

Don't the Scriptures say something about God's playing a dirty trick on Pharaoh and hardening the poor king's heart so he *could not* repent? If so, that disproves everything else!

Let's look at the evidence. In Exodus 4:21 we read that the Lord said, "I will harden his heart, so that he will not let the people go." There are nine other similar statements, that the Lord would harden the king's heart, or make it stubborn. At first glance, it seems to be a pretty bad case against any Good News from the Lord.

But there are also ten statements that say that Pharaoh hardened his own heart. For example: "When Pharaoh saw that there was relief [temporary relief from the plagues], he hardened his heart and did not heed them, *as the Lord had said*" (Exodus 8:15). Even the heathen many years later admitted that "the Egyptians and Pharaoh hardened their hearts" (1 Samuel 6:6). When the Lord said, "I will harden his heart," He meant that He would withdraw the restraining, softening influence of His Holy Spirit and leave the king to indulge his chosen feelings of rebellion as far as he wished.

God focused His spotlight on Pharaoh to show all of us the awful reality of what we can become if we choose to resist His Holy Spirit. It's like a lump of clay in the bright sunshine. The only way to keep it soft is to keep watering it. Pharaoh was left to dry up because that's what he wanted. By rejecting God's rain, the clay of his heart was hardened. A natural process worked itself out as the result of the king's choice, in accord with universal laws that God has ordained.

The Apostle Paul Understood
What Happened to Pharaoh

"Is God to be charged with injustice? By no means. For He says to Moses, 'Where I show mercy, I will show mercy, and where I pity, I will pity.' Thus it does not depend on man's will or effort, but on God's mercy. For Scripture says to Pharaoh, 'I have raised you up for this very purpose, to exhibit My power in My dealings with you, and to spread My fame over all the world.' Thus He not only shows mercy as He chooses, but also makes men stubborn as He chooses.

"You will say, 'Then why does God blame a man? For who can resist His will?' Who are you, sir, to answer God back? Can the pot speak to the potter and say, 'Why did you make me like this?'? Surely the potter can do what he likes with the clay. Is he not free to make out of the same lump two vessels, one to be treasured, the other for common use?" (Romans 9:14-21, NEB).

Let's not put words in God's mouth that He did not say. The potter never makes a vessel *in order to break it or throw it away.* Jeremiah says that a wise potter (and surely the Lord is wise!) will not discard a vessel that gets marred on the wheel, but shapes it into something else useful. One that was originally intended to be a treasure may end up in common use (see Jeremiah 18:2-6). But it was never the Lord's plan that Pharaoh be a *lost* man, but because he chose the way of rebellion, the Lord let him become an outstanding example of what people make of themselves when they do resist the Holy Spirit. Throughout the tragedy of Pharaoh's progression from initial stubbornness to rebellion and bitterness, the Lord was patient and merciful, as Paul points out:

"What if God, desiring to exhibit His retribution at work and to make His power known, tolerated very patiently those vessels which were objects of retribution due for destruction, and did so in order to make known the full wealth of His splendour upon vessels which were objects of mercy, and which from the first had been prepared for this splendour?

"Such vessels are we, whom He has called from among Gentiles as well as Jews" (Romans 9:24, NEB).

In the judgment day Pharaoh will never shake his fist at God and say, "You programmed me to harden my heart! It's your fault!" God would quietly answer, "You could have been a vessel for splendor, but I left you to have your own way which *you* chose."

The "Good News" tells us that God has given to "every man" a complete pardon and welcome into His family; it's already his. *Let him choose to accept it.* "God ... has saved us and called us with a holy calling, ... in Christ Jesus before time began, ... who has abolished death and brought life and immortality to light through the gospel" (2 Timothy 1:8-10). We cannot rewrite Paul's words for him. Christ has "*abolished* death," he says. That is, if any human being at last suffers the pain of the second death, it will be against God's will and action because that punishment is specifically "prepared for the devil and his angels" (Matthew 25:41). Any human who gets there does so only because he thwarted God's salvation already wrought out for him, like Saul kicking against the Lord's leading, or Pharaoh hardening his own heart.

One of the Most Explosive Ideas in God's Good News Is Grace

This is kindness shown to the most undeserving. That includes everybody. That "grace of God has appeared, *bringing salvation to all men*" (Titus 2:11, NASB).

There are various translations of this passage that differ significantly from this rendering because some translators can't fathom how good the Good News is. However, that *New American Standard Bible* is true to the original meaning. Paul also said: "It follows, then, that as the issue of one misdeed [Adam's] was condemnation for all men, so the issue of one just act [Christ's sacrifice of Himself on the cross] is acquittal and life for all men" (Romans 5:18, NEB).

The *King James Version* says: "The free gift came upon all men unto justification of life." There are four ways by which people have tried to understand this text:

1. *The "justification" means what it says, but the "all men" doesn't mean what it says.* Christ died only for the elect. This is Calvinist predestination and must deny what the apostle said.

2. *The "all men" means what it says, but the "acquittal" or "justification" don't mean what they say.* Christ only made a *provision*

for justification or acquittal, while He keeps the cards stacked against "all men" like a prosecuting attorney, until they do something good first. But this also must contradict the gospel.

3. *The "all men" means what it says, and the "justification" means what it says: therefore everybody is going to be saved whether or not they want to be.* This is Universalism, but the rest of the Bible contradicts this false assumption. The sad truth is that many will be lost at last.

4. *In recent years, another understanding is beginning to take root in many hearts.* The "all men" means exactly what it says, and the "justification" means exactly what it says: acquittal was *effected* at the cross for everybody. But this acquittal can be resisted, rejected, and reversed by the perverse choice of the sinner not to believe. *This has to be the true Bible understanding of this passage.*

Could Paul's Enthusiasm Have Outstripped His Common Sense?

In case you are tempted to think that this "News" is just too good, let us see what Jesus Himself has to say. "God so loved the world that He gave His only begotten Son, that whoever believes in Him should not perish … but that *the world* through Him might be saved" (John 3:16, 17). His blood was "shed for *many*" (Matthew 26:28). He gave His "flesh … for the life of *the world*" (John 6:51). The Samaritans said He is "the Savior of *the world*" (4:42).

"Ah, yes," says someone, "you see the catch? You've got to do something terribly difficult for most of us—you've got to *believe*. God pretends to be ever so generous, but He still has His loophole; He keeps the cards stacked against those 'many.' They must do something first!"

What More Could God Do?

The *King James Version* offers an encouraging answer to this objection: "God *hath dealt to every man* the measure of faith" (Romans 12:3).

If God handed out this "measure" arbitrarily, it would confirm the predestination libel against His character, for He would be handing out tickets to Heaven to His favorites and slamming the door in the face of others. But not only has He given the Savior to "every man," but with the gift He has also added "the measure of faith" to receive Him. This means that everybody becomes responsible for what he does with the gift of salvation already placed in his hands. "It is by grace you have been saved, through faith—and this not from yourselves, it is the gift of God" (Ephesians 2:8, NIV).

It follows therefore that the only way anyone can be lost is to reject that gift given by grace so freely. "Here lies the test: the light has come into the world, but men preferred darkness to light" (John 3:19, NEB). This "preference," says Jesus, involves personal choice. In other words, no one can be lost because of his past sins, for God has provided and given justification for us all. The lost reject it, having *preferred* to hang on to sin.

This "preference" may be a series of unconscious choices, but the judgment will at last disclose how each lost individual has again and again spurned that Light that brightened his or her dark soul.

All along the road that leads to death there are pains and penalties, sorrows and disappointments, warnings not to go on. God's *agape* has made it hard for the heedless and headstrong to destroy themselves. More than this, by the Holy Spirit the Savior is sitting beside each of us as we travel down that Freeway in the wrong direction, constantly nudging us to get into the right lane and take that blessed exit ramp to life eternal. His job is to be a *parakletos*, "one called to the side of" us and to constantly "convict" us of "sin and righteousness and judgment" (John 16:8, NIV). He will never tire of His job or leave us to our perverse ways unless we beat Him off persistently the same way Pharaoh did. Pharaoh is our lesson-book in how to be lost.

An old song says something true:

> And once again the scene was changed,
>   new earth there seemed to be,
> I saw the Holy City beside the tideless sea.
>
> The light of God was on its streets,
>   the gates were open wide,
> And all who would might enter,
>   and no one was denied.
> —*The Holy City*, by Frederick Weatherly, 1892

In other words, God is voting *for you*. He has elected us all to be saved. Our job is to say, Yes, to believe, to let our hearts be softened by the sweet influence of the Holy Spirit, to show appreciation for the love by which we were redeemed.

The Lord Is a Divine Gentleman

Remember, of course, the Lord will not force Himself on anyone who doesn't like Him and doesn't want Him around. He cannot use coercion. If He forced all to be saved, many would be miserable in an environment where the prevailing spirit is heartfelt gratitude to the

Lamb for His sacrifice. If by accident one rebel found himself in the City, he would head for the nearest exit.

When you see what happened at the cross, the kind of love that pushed Christ to do what He did, all this talk about it being hard to obey, hard to give all to Him, hard to surrender, hard to persevere, becomes silly. It's only our pathetic blindness in the face of the greatest Light that ever shown in all eternity that makes us imagine for a moment that we are sacrificing anything when we give all for Christ. Justification by faith can never produce one whit less than total obedience. Let's look again at the dimensions of that sacrifice:

> "If God is for us, who can be against us? He who did not spare His own Son, but delivered Him up for us all, how shall He not with Him also freely give us all things?" (Romans 8:31, 32).

How can we who appreciate such love not also freely give *Him* all things? Wouldn't such devotion include keeping all of His commandments, including the Lord's true Sabbath even if the world disregards it? Any vestige of a self-caring motivation by withholding full obedience, will negate the truth of justification by faith. It has to, for it cancels out faith. If I withhold from Christ full obedience to any one of His commandments which contain "the whole duty of man," I program myself to stand before Him at last with downcast eyes in shame, for I will never be able to forget how He withheld nothing in His utter devotion for me. For one who accepts God's Good News, obedience that once may have seemed impossible becomes now a joyous principle.

The Good News Works!

It will accomplish something never yet done since time began: it will prepare a people from all over the world to be ready for Christ's glorious appearing. There will be no faces downcast with shame in that vast throng. To have let the Lord do something *for them*, and *in them*, will be looked upon as their greatest joy.

You can know today that you are expected to be there among the happy ones, not as a guest, but as one belonging to the Establishment. Heaven's computers are spelling out your name as one predestined to be saved. Even though there are so many billions of people on planet Earth, you don't have to be content with the fraction of one billionth part of God's loving attention. You get the whole of it, for He is infinite. It's like standing outside in the bright sunshine; you get as much as if you were the only person on earth. If you will simply believe it, you are like an only child to your heavenly Father.

If anyone cancels God's will for his salvation, *He* will feel the pain of the rejection even more than the sinner does. John the Revelator says that when the Lamb had "opened the seventh seal, there was silence in heaven" (Revelation 8:1).

That mystic quietness will be the first time since all eternity that silence has overtaken the music-filled vaults of the universe. Could that be the silence of God's infinite grief as He mourns for those who have insisted on *dis*-believing His Good News and thus choosing for themselves the way of self-destruction?

Your Personal Notes

For the grace of God that brings salvation has appeared to all men, teaching us that, denying ungodliness and worldly lusts, we should live soberly, righteously, and godly in the present age, looking for the blessed hope and glorious appearing of our great God and Savior Jesus Christ, who gave Himself for us, that He might redeem us from every lawless deed and purify for Himself His own special people, zealous for good works (Titus 2:11-14).

7

God Saves Even Prostitutes If ...

(He does indeed if they don't stop Him)

Reputed to be in the oldest profession, prostitutes are singled out in the Bible for considerable attention. They get a bad press, but also a good one. Uncomplimentary things are said about them, but there is also an item of very good news about them: when John the Baptist came preaching his version of the Good News, Jesus said "the prostitutes believed Him" (Matthew 21:32, GNB).

That's a mark in their favor. It's more than the Pharisees did!

This meant, Jesus said, that those "prostitutes are going into the Kingdom of God" (verse 31). The point is that very great sinners can believe the Good News and when they do, they are transformed by it.

It would do us all good to study the case history of one woman especially. She was of questionable ethics, but she received from Jesus the *summa cum laude*—Mary Magdalene. He spoke more highly of her than of any other sinner in history—that wherever the Gospel is proclaimed throughout the whole world, her story must be told with it. This chapter therefore is dedicated to her.

Mary's Story Illustrates Two Vital Truths

1. The love of Christ can reach the most apparently hopeless person.

2. The definition of faith *which works* is a heartfelt appreciation of what it cost the Savior to save us.

Piecing together the vital facts about Mary as found here and there in the four Gospels, we learn that she had earned the title "a sinner" (Luke 7:37), a euphemistic way of saying that she was known as a lady of ill repute. In fact, she had fallen so low that she was practically a basket case. Two Gospel writers characterize her as having been possessed with "seven demons" (Luke 8:2; Mark 16:9).

The noted endocrinologist, Dr. Robert B. Greenblatt, in his *Search the Scriptures*, suggests that "Mary of Magdala may well have suffered from a compulsive neurosis known as *nymphomania*. … Mary was a woman of rank and means; how else could she afford the expensive alabaster box of ointment which she brought to anoint the feet of Jesus?" (page 93). This woman had somehow drifted beyond the bounds of self-control. How she got that way is an interesting detail of the New Testament story.

Looking at the evidence, we see that the woman who anointed Jesus' feet in Luke 7:37, 38 was the same one described by John as Mary of Bethany, the sister of Martha (John 11:1, 2), and the Mary Magdalene of Mark 16:9 as the one "out of whom [Jesus] had cast seven demons." All the details of the mosaic fit together beautifully.

This means that Mary came from a good home in one of Jerusalem's better suburbs. Her brother was the highly respected Lazarus, and her sister Martha had earned a reputation for being a super hostess in good society.

Mary probably had as happy a childhood as any girl in Judea. All went well until Simon the Pharisee seduced her. Thoughtful people have identified him as a member of her family, which would mean that what got her started going the wrong way was incest. Jesus' parable in Luke 7:40-47 clearly implicates him as the man who had originally ruined her life.

Simon, who outwardly was a respected member of the clergy known as Pharisees, secretly was a Don Juan wolf in sheep's clothing—a breed that has never become wholly extinct. How the evil act took place, we are not told. However, it is known that girls who are led this way regularly lose their self-respect and frequently are plagued by severe inner problems. It's also common in such cases for the woman to keep the secret locked up in her heart, where the poison gnaws away.

In this case Simon apparently kept the secret, too. After all, he had a high reputation as a religious leader to preserve.

What Could Mary Do?

Judean social circles had a very little redemptive concern for a girl who had gotten caught in such a tragedy. Mary probably had no chance to get good pastoral counseling. Who among the clergy would believe her story? Her seducer was a highly respected religious leader. What could she do?

It seems that Mary earned her title of "Magdalen" by having run away to the village of Magdala in Galilee—as far from home as she could go. As often happens in such cases, where no one cares, Mary in despair threw all caution to the winds. Her nosedive took her into depths of degradation in which sordid spirits from the abyss ruled her mind and soul. She was a goner, and no one could guess why this fine, intelligent girl plunged to the nadir of immorality. All her self-respect was shattered.

Then It Was Her Good Fortune to Come in Contact With Jesus

Disillusioned and bitter about men (injured women generally are!), she found something different in Him. He was fully human, for He had taken upon Himself our flesh and nature. She probably did not realize who He was for some time. He could be the Son of God incognito. He cared for her—that she felt; but it dawned on her that His love was not a designing self-interest. Here was a purity that she never had dreamed existed.

His influence on her awakened girlhood dreams. She was more than a thing to be discarded; she was a person. Could she who had fallen so low become a daughter in God's family? Strange little shoots of hope began to blossom in the spring sunshine of a Savior's pure-hearted love. Jesus began building at the right foundation. He rebuilt her self-respect.

With being possessed of seven demons, no psychiatric treatment could help her like a prayer of Jesus. She heard Him pour out His soul in impassioned pleadings for her deliverance.

Prayer saved her. She became free.

All went well for a time, but temptation apparently caught her off guard, and she fell. And no fall hurts so much as the one that comes after you think you are converted.

The Humanness of This Woman

Mary felt devastated. Despair threw her right back where she had been. But again Jesus prayed for her, and again she was delivered. And then again she fell. This seems to have gone on and on. She was the classic "new convert," which staid and cynical church members repeatedly say won't last.

Christ's disciples obviously lost all patience with her—this is evident from the way Mark tells the story. One can almost hear them advising Jesus, "Let her go—she's had it. Don't waste any more time on her!"

But the seventh time Jesus prayed for her, she was delivered. That last demon was cast out, the last root of unbelieving despair eliminated.

The mind and heart that had been a habitation of demons found genuine and lasting deliverance in believing Good News about herself and about her Savior, instead of the Bad News that had caused her such darkness of mind.

You Can't Blame Mary for Wanting to
Say "Thank You" in Some Tangible Way

Figuratively, she had been to hell and come back, and her new obsession was how to show her gratitude to her Deliverer.

Realizing distinctly what she had been saved *from*, and what she had been saved *to*, Mary's soul blossomed into the full meaning of discipleship. Henceforth no measured, restrained, "balanced" devotion would do for her. Our common "neither cold nor hot" lukewarmness became forever impossible for this daughter of Bethany. Something began brewing in her soul that would shatter for all time and eternity our restricted concepts of human capacity for devotion. Mary was on the way to earning world respect as a special person, but in a way to humble our human pride as nothing but Calvary has ever done.

She had picked up some snatches of conversation which the Twelve seem to have missed in their common preoccupation to secure the highest place in the kingdom. Jesus told them He was to die, and He repeated this to them on several occasions. But they wouldn't let the thought stay in their minds. You remember, Peter had rebuked Him for even thinking of dying.

But Mary had something called prescience; at least, she had ears to listen to what the Lord had said. Knowing that He was going to die, she wanted to do something to show her gratitude for delivering her from her life of utter darkness—but there seemed to be no way.

Well, she could at least prepare His body for death!

The shopkeeper who sold ointment for the dead could be expected to offer her a special as a bargain, not knowing of course what she had in mind. One can hear her asking, "Have you something better?"

"Yes, but you can't afford it, Mary; it's for very wealthy people."

"Let me have it," she replies. But before paying the price, she asks again, "Have you something still better?"

Stunned, the apothecary would naturally ask, "Who do you want this for? I do have one 'alabaster jar of perfume' that is intended for a king. It's the finest in the world, maybe for King Herod someday, or Governor Pilate, or possibly—who knows?—the great Caesar overseas. It's imported from the Himalayas, and costs a fortune—three hundred *denarii*, the silver coins representing a working man's wage for a full year" (see Matthew 20:1, 2).

"That's a fortune! Forget it, Mary; take my bargain special."

"No, I want the best," she says, and pays the price, possibly her life savings.

We don't know how long she dreamed and brooded over her secret scheme to show her love for the Savior. But she still wasn't satisfied. Anoint His *dead* body? He'd never know of her gratitude that way. What could she *do*?

Simon Re-enters the Picture

Then came a day when Simon the great Pharisee would throw a feast in honor of Jesus. He had never been happy since his affair with Mary. Men also know what guilt and shame are, even though they try to hide their remorse. Simon felt a sting of guilt that only the seducer can know better than the seduced. There was no one he could talk to about it, and the poison had penetrated deep into his soul.

Trying to repress his guilt, Simon put on a brave front as a respected religious leader, like King David going about his royal business after his affair with Bathsheba and his murder of her husband. But the inward burden weighed so heavy that Simon's health broke. Often carrying a hidden load of guilt will do that to us, which is why that weakest organ of our body breaks down.

The great Simon succumbed to leprosy, then universally regarded as the curse of God. Tortured with remorse and now feeling that God had forever forsaken him, Simon as a leper was a wreck of a man.

But then he too had been fortunate enough to meet up with Jesus, and the Savior had cleansed him of his leprosy.

Reserved and cautious about honoring the Man his fellow Pharisees despised, Simon sought a way to say thanks to his Benefactor through polite outward amenities. Hence the social feast at his house, with Jesus and His disciples the guests of honor.

Mary Crashes the Gate

She came, working her way in uninvited, a new and secret idea birthed in her soul. Bringing her "alabaster jar of perfume," she would anoint the Savior while He was still living!

Pressing in to the dining room unobserved, she impulsively broke the seal on the precious flask of ointment, anointing His head while He reclined at the table, and then evidently pouring the rest of it over His feet. As the rich and unusual ointment ran to waste on the floor, its fantastic fragrance suddenly filled the room. The buzz of conversation ceased, and all eyes turned to discover what had happened.

Mary was sobbing, a hidden fountain of grateful tears burst open. She seemed driven to her deed. A language beyond words was pouring forth in tears—"Thank You, Lord, for saving my soul!" She had not thought to bring a towel (only fussy Martha would plan so carefully), so she took His feet in her hands and dried them with her long flowing hair which she had shamelessly let down.

It was as a catharsis to her. At last her pent up soul had found expression. She probably didn't realize that she was center stage by now and was unprepared for what was coming.

Mark respectfully tells us that "some" became angry at her deed, but politely he doesn't tell us who they were. We are left wondering if they might have been the Gentile guests present. But no, Matthew "spills the beans" and tells us frankly that the critics were none other than the ordained disciples of Jesus. And then John completes the story by telling us that these ridiculous complaints were coming from that supposedly wonderful man that everybody thought was a star—Judas Iscariot, the savvy businessman disciple of Jesus.

"Why this waste of perfume? It could have been sold for more than a year's wages and the money given to the poor," Judas is ranting. Mark tells us that the Eleven got caught up in his complaints and readily seconded his motion of censure: "And they rebuked her harshly" (Mark 14:4, 5, NIV). Think of it, Jesus' own disciples had no patience with this woman.

Mary Was Devastated

The sweetness in her soul was about to turn to the gall of disappointment. Yes, why hadn't she thought to sell her precious ointment, and make a more magnificent gift for Judas, the honorable treasurer of the group? Come to think of it, Jesus had indeed many times pleaded for the cause of the poor. That *would* have been a better idea! Oh, why hadn't she thought of it?

In her embarrassment and humiliation, she was about to bolt for the door, but Jesus' words caught her and held her: "Leave her alone," He said, probably looking Judas square in the eye. (There's no record that He had ever previously rebuked Judas, as He had often rebuked Peter.) "She has done a beautiful thing to Me. The poor you will always have with you, and you can help them any time you want. But you will not always have Me. She did what she could" (Mark 14:6-8, NIV). "When she poured this perfume on My body, she did it to prepare Me for burial" (Matthew 26:12, NIV).

As in a dream, Mary heard the commendation. This was no half-hearted gesture in her behalf. Jesus' whole soul was aroused, and He rebuked Judas and the Eleven with a passion they would never forget. In fact, Judas was so stung by the rebuke that he left the party determined to betray Him (see Matthew 26:14-16).

70

Why Did Jesus Praise Her So Highly?

He read and warmly appreciated the secret purposes of Mary's soul—she had prepared Him for His burial. She, "a sinner," had anointed the body of the Son of God, and had given Him a perfumed memory to carry in His heart through the darkness of Gethsemane and right on up to Calvary, until that last conscious moment when He should cry out, "It is finished!"

No angel could do as much. Let Satan wring His soul with fierce temptations as He hung on His cross. Why give Your life a ransom for these unfeeling, ungrateful humans? Look, Your own people have despised and rejected You; one of Your chosen Twelve has betrayed You; another has denied You with most unpious cursing and swearing; all have forsaken You and fled. Wipe the bloody sweat from Your brow and come down from that horrible cross. If You are the Son of God, You can! Why waste Yourself like this?

We may never sense how almost overmastering that temptation was to the divine-human Savior in His weakest moment.

But then there steals into His consciousness a fragrant memory: the anointing by the daughter of Bethany. Here was *one* whose human soul had been stretched outsize to appreciate His outsized sacrifice. The offering on Calvary may seem wasted for the many millions of planet earth, even perhaps for the Eleven (or so it seemed temporarily); but it is worthwhile for Mary Magdalene, the fallen soul. The sacrifice of God in Christ has elicited from one sinner its true complementary sacrifice—"a broken spirit, a broken and a contrite heart," which God, unlike the disciples, will "not despise" (Psalm 51:17).

Mary Anointed *Him* to His cross, Not Just His Body

What an honor for her! We owe to the Virgin Mary the human birth of our Lord; but perhaps we owe to this other Mary a debt of gratitude for encouraging His tempted soul in the crucial hour of His sacrifice when the fate of the world trembled in the balance.

Jesus' encomium of praise was His *summa cum laude* bestowed on this redeemed soul. It seems to border on extravagance: "I tell you the truth, wherever the gospel is preached throughout the world, what she has done will also be told, in memory of her" (Mark 14:9, NIV). Something is driving us, even in this chapter, to fulfill that prophecy. What she did was "beautiful," Jesus said (Greek *kalos*, fantastically neat, brilliantly conceived, gorgeous). Mary has preached a sermon that will reverberate to earth's ends and even be remembered in eternity. Not even Peter at Pentecost was half so eloquent.

Such are the immeasurable results that flow when one apparently hopeless person makes a choice to *believe* the Good News.

8

God Saves Even
Self-righteous People If ...

(He loves them just as much!)

It surprises us, but it's true—the Bible teaches that God has a comparatively easy time saving repentant prostitutes and self-confessed criminals. His most difficult task is saving "saints" who have forgotten that they are sinners.

There are plenty of these, church-goers who may never have "fallen" as did Mary Magdalene or King David, but whose hearts have become calcified. They have held on to the dangerous idea that they are pretty good people in themselves and can't see why they need repentance. (At least not like "bad" people do.)

What makes it difficult for the Lord to help such "saints" is that they feel no need. Worse still, they have gotten beyond feeling truly thankful for Jesus' sacrifice. This is to be expected; they feel they deserve salvation by being more righteous than the wicked.

Now comes the Good News that Jesus can find a way to help even such lost "saints." He knows how to penetrate the shell they have built up around themselves, unaware of their true condition. We discover this Good News in the story of how Jesus handled Simon the Pharisee at his party.

Something Good Had Already Happened to Mary

Her heart had undeniably been changed, but Simon's was still like a stone. Jesus assured her directly, "Your sins are forgiven" (Luke 7:48, NIV). Then He added one more thing, a lesson that will stop us cold in our tracks, if we'll just let His point sink in.

In a lightning flash illumination, Jesus revealed something that for nearly two thousand years theologians have debated and argued: *what is faith?* Jesus defined it when He said to Mary, "Your *faith* has saved you; go in peace" (verse 50, NIV). *What Mary had is true faith.*

When Do You and I Dare to Claim That We Have Faith?

In effect, Jesus' answer is this: only when we have what Mary Magdalene had—a heart-moving appreciation of the love of Christ. Nothing less is worthy of the name, because nothing less can melt our hard hearts.

"You mean I must run the gamut of abandonment like she did, and virtually go to hell first?" No, for you may never find your way back like she did. But we can have *the faith* that Mary had, if we will simply realize the truth that were it not for the grace of Christ, hell itself is the only dimension of the ruin we would know.

Not one of us is innately any more righteous than Mary was in her lostness. Not one is saved part way by Christ—He saves 100 percent, or not at all. If all the unknown factors that have shaped our lives were realized, we would see that *we are Mary.* Our coldness is the consequence of our not knowing the truth about ourselves and about Him.

Simon the Pharisee was afflicted with that blind ignorance, a condition worse than his former leprosy. How could Jesus reach him? If it is true that Jesus "was in all points tempted as we are" (Hebrews 4:15), we can assume that He was tempted to sigh and say to Himself, Mary has made it, but I'll just abandon this hopeless man; he is too difficult to reach. We can be grateful that Jesus decided to do something to help even him.

Can We Learn the Secret of How Jesus Saved Simon?

The Savior must have gotten up early that morning to pray and ask His Father for wisdom for all the problems He would meet that day. Note how the Father answered His prayer:

Simon saw all that Mary had done in anointing Jesus and had heard His words of appreciation for her. He couldn't help taking it all in. But very dark thoughts were coursing through this "respectable" man's mind.

Having witnessed the most beautiful deed ever performed by a repentant sinner, the best this poor soul could do was to congratulate himself on his own savvy for not accepting Jesus as his Messiah and Savior. Luke tells the story (see Luke 7:36-47, NIV):

"When the Pharisee who had invited him saw this, he said to himself, 'If this man were a prophet, he would know who is touching him and what kind of woman she is—that she is a sinner.'" I *know* this woman, Simon said to himself. Genuine prophets associate with better people than she is! My fellow Pharisees surely are right—Jesus of Nazareth must be a phony!

His reverie is interrupted by his Guest. "Simon, I have something to tell you."

"Tell me, Teacher." He has to be polite.

"Two men owed money to a certain moneylender. One owed him five hundred *denarii* [silver coins], and the other fifty. Neither of them had the money to pay him back, so he canceled the debts of both. Now which of them will love him more?"

Simon was probably too intelligent not to realize that the Savior was groping for some way to reach his heart. He had to respond, "I suppose the one who has the bigger debt canceled." Could a ray of light already have pierced this poor man's darkened soul? Could he be on the way to seeing how he was the greater sinner of the two?

"You have judged correctly," Jesus assured him. He probably gave the uncomfortable man a knowing look that told him that his Guest understood all. The divine Surgeon must operate, but He will wield His scalpel very skillfully and mercifully.

Jesus did something strange. It appears that He turned His back on Simon now, for "He turned toward the woman" while He continued to address Simon. "Do you see this woman? I came into your house. You did not give me any water for my feet." Simon, think! You were too ashamed of Me before your fellow Pharisees to show the elemental courtesy of having your servant wash My travel-weary feet with ordinary water, or even give Me some to do it Myself. But this woman whom you despise— "she wet my feet with her tears and wiped them with her hair."

But this is not all.

"You did not give me a kiss," like you do your peers; "but this woman, from the time I entered, has not stopped kissing my feet." The Master probably paused, to give this time to probe Simon's conscience, now burning like fire.

Jesus went on: "You did not put oil on My head," not even a teaspoonful of the cheapest variety, for something like that is always accorded guests of honor; "but she has poured perfume on My feet," of such a quality that you have heard how our financial expert Judas Iscariot has reckoned its astonishing monetary value.

Mary is still kneeling. All seven demons are gone now, no trace left even of bitterness toward Simon for what he had done to her. He can doubtless sense the reality of her forgiveness of him, which makes it easier for him at last to receive God's forgiveness.

Jesus didn't need to slash Simon's miserable heart with the public announcement that He knew how he was the incestuous seducer. By now Simon himself is frantically computing the difference between owing five hundred *denarii* and owing only fifty.

He begins to realize that he is in the presence of One whose love and compassion are infinite. His Guest could have walked out on him in high dudgeon, manifesting a much-deserved contempt. Thanks, Simon, for inviting me; but I have to leave before the dessert. Goodbye!

No. Simon can be inexpressibly thankful that Jesus did not mercilessly expose him to his guests; any ordinary prophet, such as Nathan before King David or Elijah before Ahab, could well have humiliated him. Some therapeutic tears could already be trickling down Simon's face as he hears the Savior add, "Therefore, I tell you, her many sins have been forgiven—for she loved much. But he who has been forgiven little loves little" (see Luke 7:37-47, NIV). The principle holds true in all ages.

The Good News That Hurt,
But Also Healed

Love drove the point home with the force of a sledgehammer. Simon began to see his condition as he had never seen it before. Despising the woman who had been troubled by seven demons, he now saw himself possessed of an eighth—a self-righteousness and hypocrisy that now suddenly appears abhorrent to him. A Savior's infinite love has turned a double tragedy (tragedies are seldom single!) into a dual conversion.

When Jesus said to Simon, "Do you see this woman?" He was in effect setting her forth as a demonstration of what it means to be truly saved. While it is true that we are saved only by faith, not always has faith itself been intelligently understood. Mary provides us with its true definition. In a very real sense, this formerly dissolute woman sympathized "with Christ" in His grand sacrifice. The content of her faith was the heart fellowship she knew with Christ in His sacrifice; that enabled her to reflect His.

Why Did Jesus Praise Mary So Highly?

Jesus saw something that Mary could not see. He foretold for her memory the worldwide proclamation of her deed until the end of time, because it illuminated in a special way His deed in our behalf. I used to wonder why Jesus was so enthusiastic in His praise of Mary. It involved a sharp rebuke to Judas and even to the Eleven who joined him in his criticism of her. Why didn't He soothe the ruffled feelings around the table by praising Mary a bit more conservatively? *I* would have; wouldn't you?

He could have said something like this in order to make peace all around: Mary, I appreciate your desire to say "thanks" for saving your soul, but really—now don't cry—Judas and the disciples are right in principle. Think of all the poor people those three hundred silver coins could have helped. You could have spent say ten (that would be a lot!) on a mere spoonful of ointment for anointing My head (never mind My feet), and then you could have brought the 290 *denarii* into our treasury, so Judas our honorable treasurer could have dispensed it to the poor. I know you meant well, Mary, and I give you credit for good intentions, but next time you'll know better, won't you? Now, there, … don't cry.

No way! He praised her to the skies. She is lifted up as His model follower. No one else had eyes to see her strange, apparently irrational act as He saw it. He was intensely happy that at last here was someone who at least was beginning to appreciate what He was doing.

- In the broken alabaster jar lying discarded on the floor, He saw an emblem of His body to be broken for us and laid in the tomb.
- In the precious ointment running to waste all over the floor, He saw an emblem of His blood shed sufficient to save an entire world, yet only a mere handful of its inhabitants appreciating it.
- What He saw as astoundingly "beautiful" in Mary's deed was the magnificence of her offering. It was reckless in its prodigality.

Oh, that any sinful human being on this fallen planet should conceive of doing such a beautiful thing! It mirrored the overwhelming prodigality of Christ's sacrifice for us. Love is never love unless it is magnificently prodigal. A cup of the water of life may be enough to save our souls, but Christ must pour it out a veritable Niagara, enough to save all of earth's billions. According to Jesus' evaluation, the woman once possessed of "seven demons" has unwittingly become the most eloquent evangelist of all time.

Poor Simon Must Sit and Learn From Her

Luke draws the curtain on the drama as Simon sits there pondering Mary's faith that saved her. We never hear from him again. But we can be sure that our Lord's loving ministry in behalf of this lost man was not in vain. Surely the proud Pharisee became a lowly, self-sacrificing disciple.

Simon the Pharisee became the pioneer success example for other self-righteous souls who are the most difficult for Christ to reach.

Unless they find what Simon found, they will be the tragic figures whom Jesus describes:

> "Many will say to me on that day, 'Lord, Lord, did we not prophesy in your name, and in your name drive out demons and perform many miracles?' Then I will tell them plainly, 'I never knew you.'" "I was hungry and you gave me nothing to eat, I was thirsty and you gave me nothing to drink, I was a stranger and you did not invite me in, I needed clothes and you did not clothe me, I was sick and in prison and you did not look after me" (Matthew 7:22, 23; 25:42, 43, NIV).

The miracle that redeemed Simon the Pharisee could have been a greater one than the redemption of Mary. But it was done; and that is *superb* Good News.

There is hope for all of us if ... , if we will "listen" to Mary's eloquent, visual sermon.

9

The Grass May Not Be
Greener on the Other Side

(There is Good News for
many difficult marriages)

One of the most devastating items of Bad News is the feeling
that you have married the wrong spouse; your marriage is
doomed to be unhappy.

This "realization" is bitter as gall. Does the Bible offer any practical
Good News to heal a hurt like this?

No one can deny that plenty of people are hurting. Conservative
estimates say that roughly half of marriages are doomed statistically to
end in breakups; and those who don't divorce but grit their teeth to
endure marital misery is a good proportion of the remainder. When
you drive by and admire beautiful houses and well-manicured lawns,
you can know that precious few of those palaces are happy inside.

No end of "secrets" and prescriptions for happiness in marriage
are published in a flood of books and magazine articles. But there is a
method of healing that seems not to get on to the talk shows. It's not a
program of things to do, or techniques to memorize and remember. It's
this simple idea: *Believe God's Good News about your marriage.*

There is some. It would be foolish to predict 100 percent success in
every difficulty, but in many cases, happiness can be realized.

That Good News May Well Be
Better Than You Think It Is

Terminating your present marriage and getting into a new one may
not be the solution it seems to be, even though you may be strongly
tempted to think it is your only possible path to happiness.

I well realize that some who have divorced and remarried say they are supremely happy in their new union. I would not utter a word to lessen their present happiness, or to threaten their new relationship. But God has revealed in His word that till-death-do-us-part marriage is His preferred way of happiness. There's a reason; it's not just His arbitrary decision.

He is gracious and kind to those who have suffered the misfortune of a marital breakup, and this is why some remarry happily. But the facts are that a far greater percentage of divorced people never achieve the subsequent happiness they hoped for.

Some people can drink moderately and manage to control it, but a good percentage of "moderate" drinkers end up with the problem. The same can be said for smoking. Some smoke all their lives and survive to be a hundred; but many develop lung cancer, emphysema, or cardiac problems. This is why love and common sense suggest that the safest, wisest thing is to neither drink nor smoke at all. Likewise, a few divorce-success stories may be lethally counterfeit "good news" for you.

What Good News could possibly lurk beneath the discouraging shadows of an unhappy marriage? The spiritual gloom seems so pervasive that it's like an injection of a nerve-paralyzing chemical. Not a ray of sunshine seems evident. Almost everywhere you turn, the media, TV dramas, novels, the counsel of friends, even sometimes the example of the pastor in the church and the life experiences of elders and deacons, all seem to reinforce the idea: divorce is the only possible solution.

The Marriage Counselor Who Doesn't Charge a Fee

Now is when one needs a visit with Him who is called the "Wonderful Counselor" (Isaiah 9:6). He has elected to communicate His counsel in the Bible, which anyone who can read is competent to study for himself. But there are truths therein not usually discerned. What we find will probably be quite different from what the "wise" world will advise, because "the wisdom of this world is foolishness with God. For it is written, … 'The Lord knows the thoughts of the wise, that they are futile'" (1 Corinthians 3:19, 20). God's true wisdom will unfailingly be genuine Good News, the kind that will ensure maximum happiness not only throughout life, but for eternity as well.

The wisdom of the world is Bad News on practically all counts. Conservative statistics indicate that when about a million American couples divorce annually, in most cases that means at the very least *two* million people are miserable, for although divorce may bring temporary or illusory "happiness" to one of the two, it usually brings misery to the other.

Friends and relatives are touched by the pain as well. Another million will desert their spouses without benefit of divorce; and this adds up to at least three million pained people, and probably more. An additional million couples will decide to stumble along in the agonies of incompatibility, holding together for the sake of children or relatives, but psychologically divorced. And these are where the annual statistics hover.

The saddest news of all concerns the children—another three million "innocent," usually unhappy people. Offspring from broken homes are statistically three times more likely to repeat divorces when they grow up. When kids find unhappiness at home, whether it's the result of a divorce or unhappily married parents, many find their way into the drug culture, and nearly all start off with negative expectations concerning their marriages. These youth are often described as a social time bomb, set to go off in a future decade. Some actually turn to crime and even terrorism. When the tender emotions of children are trampled, the youth often become desperate, and the juvenile courts wonder why.

Altogether, the Cost in Misery of Broken Homes Is Enormous

Not the least is the hopeless loneliness many survivors endure—down to their last days sitting forlornly in nursing homes, staring empty hearted at blank walls or TV screens until death mercifully releases them. After the passion fires of youth are banked in old age, it's nice to have someone who still loves you in a till-death-do-us-part commitment. If you turn out to be one of those fortunate few, you can thank the Savior with fervency, for you have reaped the sweet fruit of believing at least some of His Good News.

We can note at least some Bible news regarding marriage as follows:

1. *When God joins a man and wife together, He makes them become "one" for life*. The following words were spoken by Christ Himself, His own priceless comment on this subject: "Haven't you read … that … the Creator 'made them male and female,' and said, 'For this reason a man will leave his father and mother and be united to his wife, and the two will become one flesh'? So they are no longer two, but one. Therefore what God has joined together, let man not separate" (Matthew 19:4-6, NIV).

2. *Further Good News is that God who does the joining together is very powerful, stronger than the enemy of love*. Therefore God is concerned for the happiness of every married couple. Since He is the One who invented the idea of sex and marriage, He has a vested interest in the success of each marriage; otherwise He gets the blame for inventing

a bad idea. (This is probably the real reason why Satan is trying so hard to wreck modern marriages; it's one of his most effective ways of getting at God.) This leads us to another astounding Good News idea:

3. *If we have understood Jesus' words correctly, a marriage cannot break up unless one or both of the two parties puts it "asunder"* (KJV). A marriage must be *willfully* dismantled. It never falls apart of itself. As long as God has His way, it will never disintegrate. From this it would not be difficult to conclude that divorce is often a tug of war with God.

Immediately the question will arise: "Suppose *I* am not the one who is breaking up my marriage—it's my spouse who is fighting against me and God! Now what do I do?"

4. *The first thing is to believe that God is stronger than your spouse.* One marriage partner who truly believes in God (we must understand what genuine faith is!) makes a case of two against one.

5. *Scripture seems to indicate that this two-against-one approach to dealing with a troubled marriage will often mean a victory for God and the believer.*

Says an inspired apostle:

> "To the married I give this command (not I, but the Lord): A wife must not separate from her husband. But if she does, she must remain unmarried or else be reconciled to her husband. And a husband must not divorce his wife.
>
> "To the rest I say this (I, not the Lord): If any brother has a wife who is not a believer and she is willing to live with him, he must not divorce her. And if a woman has a husband who is not a believer and he is willing to live with her, she must not divorce him. For the unbelieving husband has been sanctified through his [believing] wife, and the unbelieving wife has been sanctified through her believing husband. ...
>
> "How do you know, wife, whether you will save your husband? Or, how do you know, husband, whether you will save your wife?" (1 Corinthians 7:10-16, NIV).

The apostle doesn't answer his question, leaving it to us.

6. *Not only this: the inspired apostle writes suggesting the definite hope that a believing spouse may perhaps "save" the unbelieving one.* If words mean what they say, the Bible is consistent. In the Old Testament God says, "I hate divorce" (Malachi 2:16, NIV), and the Lord's "command" in the New Testament is equally firm against it.

According to what we just read, in a marriage between a believer and an unbeliever, the latter is "sanctified," that is, he or she stands in a different relation to God because of being married to a believer than if they were in a completely non-believer relationship. I am not trying to trivialize this divine truth, but it's something like an insurance policy that covers the spouse.

7. *In other words, God is actively drawing the unbelieving spouse to Himself simply because He has a believer in that marriage!* This is very Good News, and it could pay to believe it.

What the Root of the Difficulty May Be

Sad to say, the real problem is often that the so-called believing spouse has only a veneer of faith. Self-deception among religious people is widespread.

Consider the case of the Pious Wife. She often was so devoted to church that she went to prayer meeting and tearfully asked the church to pray that her unbelieving husband might become a believer and join the church. And the people prayed.

One Sabbath morning hubby started down the steps dressed in his best suit instead of his ordinary work clothes. His startled wife asked where he was going. "To church, with you and the children," he replied with a smile.

Out came the words before she could think: "But, darling, if you lose your job because you keep the Sabbath, how will we make the payments on the house and the new car and the new furniture?" Without a word, he went back upstairs and changed into his work clothes, and that was the end forever of his joining the church. A wife who is willing to enjoy the material benefits of her husband's ongoing unbelief can hardly be a believer. This man had felt the drawing of the Lord all those years and wanted to respond; you might say that he was "sanctified" until his "believing" wife displayed her *unbelief.*

A veneered "believing" spouse (who actually is a closet secret unbeliever) may beneath the surface desire a divorce as much as the avowed unbeliever who openly says he or she wants it. In such a case, it is accurate to say that they both are putting asunder what God has joined together.

But an unbelieving spouse who is married to one who truly believes God's glorious Good News would in all probability be more inclined to want to stay with his or her believing spouse. However, because we all have free wills, this does not inevitably happen, and Paul realistically recognizes that it may not happen. So he says: "If the unbeliever leaves, let him [or her] do so. A believing man or woman is not bound in such circumstances; God has called us to live in peace" (1 Corinthians 7:15, NIV).

A Simple First Step

Believe the Good News that God loves you too much to lead you deliberately into a marriage with the wrong person. If your marriage *seems* to be a failure, self-examination is in order. Did God lead me, or did I willfully stumble into this marriage on my own, while I turned my back on God? (This agonizing question troubles many.) We learn from the story of Isaac and Rebekah that God actually overrules or even leads two people together: "You have appointed [Rebekah] for Your servant Isaac" (Genesis 24:7, 14, 40, 44).

But even if a believer concludes that he or she has entered into marriage without divine approval, this does not mean that God actually did withdraw Himself from you. And it is by no means proof that God had nothing to do with your marriage. Let me explain:

Even if you were a rank unbeliever at that time, heady and arrogant, rebellious against the Lord and/or against your parents, God foresaw that you would later become converted and be a believer, for He knows the end from the beginning and "calls those things which do not exist as though they did" (Romans 4:17). That means that He had already taken you under His wings before you even dreamed of becoming converted!

That same chapter in Genesis reveals that God had Rebekah in mind as Isaac's happy wife before she had any such idea (24:44). And of course that means that God loves you just as much as He loved Rebekah. So, in that ray of light shining from God's word you can look upon your spouse as indeed God's will for you. And then if that's true, consider: all the devils in hell cannot destroy the happiness of your marriage if you believe what God encourages you to believe is true.

This does not mean that God "arranges" your marriage as Hindu parents do. It's your own personal experience of love that has brought the two of you together—but the God of love inspired it. It only means that His love is deeper than we had ever thought it is.

Let us not forget that God's enabling grace, working in and through the believing partner, can bring good out of a bad situation. At every step such a partner will ask: Is this the way of the Lord? God promises wisdom for those who ask this in faith (see James 1:5, 6). There are instances in which the believer who has followed this plan has been instrumental in bringing the estranged unbeliever to Christ—and both have again fallen in love with each other in the process.

Marriage Couldn't Be Fun if Both Partners Were Perfect

Probably ninety-nine out of every hundred couples discover unsuspected weaknesses and faults in their marriage partner soon after marriage. A couple with that faith in God will believe that they are well mated in spite of mutual defects.

By recognizing that no one is perfect (after all who can claim to have no faults!) and by God's grace *accepting* the other person with his or her faults and weaknesses, realizing how you have your own, it is possible to achieve domestic harmony. It often happens, as time goes on, that such couples come to realize that these adjustments have been a good experience for them both. (Let's be up front: all couples have these problems!)

When those defects or incompatibilities loom so large that you cannot see hope of ever becoming "one" as God intended you to be, you do have a serious problem. One of the most poignant of these problems is the belated realization that one's spouse is guilty of infidelity. It is generally understood that Jesus gave permission for divorce when there has been marital infidelity, called "fornication" in Matthew 19:9 (KJV). Permission, however, is not a command.

Depending on circumstances, as the innocent, believing party reviews the situation with the Searcher of hearts, he may conclude that forgiveness is the best course to pursue for all concerned.

One of the problems involved in cases of infidelity is the problem of trust. Infidelity shatters one's confidence in the guilty party, so that even when we forgive him or her, it's difficult for the innocent party again to trust the guilty one.

But even here the grace of God working in and through the believer may make a miracle possible. The innocent party can ever remember that in God's sight no one is *really* innocent. The sin that another commits, I could commit if I just take my eyes off Jesus.

Here is an example: Shirley had been unfaithful to her husband, and in despair he had hanged himself. Her sister felt like reproaching her for driving him to suicide. How *could* she do a thing like that! However, this is not the end of the story. Shirley's sister says:

"A few years later in a distant community, I found myself one day flung across my bed, weeping before God, begging Him for strength and protection from immorality. Through an exhausting, agonizing struggle, ... He showed me that I, too, had the potential to be unfaithful. ... I had come to love deeply a man with whom I worked. ... I gradually realized that ... without God's help we were headed for serious trouble. ... We daily had to resist the pull towards physical intimacy. ... It was only the Lord who saved us and resolved the problem. I knew without a doubt I could not have resisted on my own."[1]

Another Practical Step of Common Sense

The Good News is that through divine grace it is possible to resist the weaknesses of the flesh. In many cases this means physically removing oneself from the tempter's ground.

The Blessed Insight of Corporate Guilt

There are cases where two who have been made "one" by the Lord come to the place where they discover that not one but *both* in God's sight share in the guilt that threatens to break up their marriage. Unconsciously, the "innocent" one has somehow made it easier for the "guilty" one to fall into the trap of infidelity. This is a deep insight only the Holy Spirit can make plain to one who thinks he or she is innocent.

It is much easier for God's grace to work successfully to help the "guilty" one and bring him or her to repentance and restoration if the "innocent" one has come to see this precious insight of truth. Any semblance of a holier-than-thou spirit is a roadblock that makes true repentance more difficult for the spouse who has erred. Shame and guilt often drives such a one to want to run from a spouse who is "holy." Self-righteousness can be a fatal blind spot.

God's Good News has X-ray perception. If His Spirit discloses that blind spot, rejoice! The pain of such a disclosure is nothing compared to the good that can result in saving a marriage and bringing two alienated spouses together in a deeper love than they knew before.

In cases in which there has been infidelity in a marriage and the innocent party truly believes the New Testament gospel and knows the grace of contrition, God will have a better chance to work a miracle in bringing the "guilty" one to true repentance. Here is hope:

> "If someone is caught in a sin, you who are spiritual should restore him gently. But watch yourself, or you also may be tempted. Carry each other's burdens, and in this way you will fulfill the law of Christ. If anyone thinks he is something when he is nothing, he deceives himself" (Galatians 6:1-3, NIV).

---

1. *Eternity* [magazine], February 1977, pp. 27, 28.

The point is not that one's own sense of self-respect must be shattered to where he thinks he or she is "nothing." But it is a very healthful experience to realize that *apart from the grace of Christ*, we would indeed be "nothing"! That's the lesson Shirley's once self-righteous sister learned when she found herself falling in love with a man who was not her husband. Her understanding and compassion suddenly began to grow.

The Bible Says "We Are Saved By Hope" (Romans 8:24)

The possibility of the "guilty" person being "restored"—this is the hope that the New Testament offers the "innocent" one who dares to cherish faith. Even though the miracle may seldom seem to happen, it remains a possibility. Perhaps the key to success is to "restore" the wrongdoer "gently," and not in a spirit of bitter accusation or cold "holier-than-thou" indignation. It is fantastic Good News when both spouses are genuinely converted and are again made "one" through a mutual discovery of the power to be found in contrition.

Iverna Tompkins in *How to Be Happy in No Man's Land*[2] is refreshingly frank regarding her own experience of self-righteousness:

"For us to get married with the loose attitude, 'If it works, it works, and if it doesn't work I'll try again,' is to have the attitude of the unbeliever. …

"But what happens when you marry and don't make it? Maybe you didn't know how to make it. I surely didn't. I was about as wise as a dove and harmless as a serpent—I had it all mixed up.

"I married a man when I was in a backslidden condition, and while he was overseas, I bore a child and gave my heart back to the Lord. When my husband came home, I had about as much wisdom as would fit into a thimble. I sat him down and said, 'Now, listen here. Let me tell you how things are going to be. We will no longer do this and that and the other thing. You're not going to smoke in my house, because this is God's house. Don't put your beer in my refrigerator. This house is dedicated to the Lord. I won't stand for those things now, and I'm not going to raise our child in that kind of atmosphere.'

"Another child and ten rocky years later, he said, 'Goodbye, Iverna. I'm going to find somebody I can live with.' He did, and they were married, and they've lived happily ever after."

Granted, a "believer" ought not deliberately to marry an unbeliever. After all, "What fellowship has … light with darkness?" (2 Corinthians

---

2. Logos Associates, June 1, 1975.

6:14). But let us remember that that "Light … lights every man coming into the world" (John 1:9) and if the Light is shining in one's own heart, the believer who finds himself or herself "yoked together" with an unbeliever may have anointed eyes to discern that the Holy Spirit is working on the conversion of the unbeliever. It would be a tragedy to scuttle the ship as it is nearing such a harbor.

God is above all a Super Evangelist. Speaking of an unbelieving spouse, perhaps we can be pardoned for applying a verse by Edwin Markham[3] to such situations:

> He drew a circle that shut me out—
> Heretic, rebel, a thing to flout;
> But Love [God] and I had the wit to win:
> We drew a circle that took him in!

A Beautiful Example of God's Evangelistic Wisdom

It's found in Galatians 4:1-5 where we see that He treats unbelievers not as outsiders or as wolves to be shot down as soon as possible, but as wandering sons or lost sheep that haven't yet found their way home.

The figure is that of a child of the wealthy estate owner who runs about barefoot, bossed by slaves; but when he comes of age, he becomes lord of the estate. "Even so we … were children … in bondage … But when the fullness of the time had come, … we … receive[d] the adoption as sons" (4:3-5).

Happy is the spouse who believes in the Good News enough to draw a circle that takes *in* the unbelieving one, assuming that he or she is a child of God "in minority" on the way to realizing and confessing that sonship or daughtership in God's good time. That's cooperating with God in working miracles!

New Testament forgiveness, whether given by God or by a believing spouse, implies the idea of being loosed from the sin, of actually sending it away. The Greek word is *aphesi*, which means literally "bearing away." The truly forgiven person is free from the sin, and won't do it again ever.

The Only Way Anyone Can Learn to Forgive

No one *can* forgive an erring spouse unless he has first experienced Christ's forgiving grace toward himself. If God invented sex and

---

3. Edwin Markham (1852-1940), poem, "Outwitted." Markham was poet Laureate of Oregon.

marriage, He also invented the redemption that centers in the cross. Miracles don't happen unless there is a sense of the tremendous "giving for" that was involved in God's forgiveness, an appreciation of the cost expended at Calvary:

> "Be kind and compassionate to one another, forgiving each other, just as in Christ God forgave you. Be imitators of God, therefore, as dearly loved children and live a life of love [*agape*], just as Christ loved us and gave Himself up for us a fragrant offering and sacrifice to God" (Ephesians 4:32; 5:1, NIV).

In olden times, marriages were happy according as the two parties believed that *God* had brought them together, rather than their own mutual chemical or social attractions for each other. Their love for each other was rooted in their primary faith in God's leading. When they had the horse before the cart, their faith in each other grew into happy, permanent love.

Isaac, for example, never laid eyes on Rebekah until his father's servant brought her to him from Mesopotamia and was told how she was *God's* choice for him. His faith concurred with God's leading, and we read that "he loved her." In fact, Isaac and Rebekah's marriage is one of the happiest recorded in the Bible (see Genesis 24:66, 67).

You may have heard the story of the man in *Acres of Diamonds*[4] who looked all over the world for treasure, only to discover the precious gems in his own backyard. The grass on the other side of the fence may not be as green as it is on your side already.

---

4. See Appendix A, p. 101.

Your Personal Notes

For I know the thoughts that I think toward you, says the LORD, thoughts of peace and not of evil, to give you a future and a hope. Then you will call upon Me and go and pray to Me, and I will listen to you. And you will seek Me and find Me, when you search for Me with all your heart (Jeremiah 29:11-13).

10

The Best Good News of All:
The Hour of God's Judgment

*(And why it is up-to-the-minute
Good News—it's here)*

The story is told that before the days of automatic sensors, British railroad law required that bridge keepers flag down trains if a storm took out the bridge. If it was night, they must wave them down with a lantern.

One bridge keeper neglected his duty and a passenger train plunged into the river. When the case came up for trial the prosecutor asked, "Did you wave your lantern in warning?"

"Yes, I did," he answered, and he was exonerated. Later, however, he confided to one of his friends, "I'm glad he didn't ask if my lantern was lighted."

Human courts of justice seldom find it possible to discover the whole truth or weigh the motives of the accused. But a judgment must come when even secret thoughts and purposes will be revealed, "including every hidden thing, whether it is good or evil" (Ecclesiastes 12:14, NIV).

"Watergates" have a way of getting out, especially in a relatively free, democratic society. But imagine a judgment in which *everything* comes out in the open, fully exposed. This will take place when life is finished, for "it is appointed for men to die once, but after this the judgment" (Hebrews 9:27).

Looking at it from the viewpoint of a prophet, the author of the Book of Revelation describes the awesome scene:

"I saw a great white throne and Him who was seated on it. Earth and sky fled from His presence, and there was no place for them. And I saw the dead, great and small, standing before the throne, and books were opened. ... The dead were judged according to what they had done as recorded in the books" (Revelation 20:11, 12, NIV).

"Books" Are Obviously a Euphemism

Some kind of vast cosmic computer has all our information accurately stored within it, including data impossible for any man-made device to capture—thoughts and motives. Each deed or hidden purpose that conflicts with the foundation principle of the universe ("the law of liberty," James 2:12) will stand out on this computer record as evidence for a case, for Heaven's "commandment is exceedingly broad" (Psalm 119:96). The prophetic judgment scene appears calculated to warn us, and (many conclude) even to frighten us into preparation. But Christ will not coerce by fear what He would win only by love.

The One who presides is an impressive figure called "the Ancient of Days," Daniel says, before whom "a fiery stream issued and came forth" and "ten thousand times ten thousand stood before Him. The court was seated, and the books were opened" (Daniel 7:9, 10). The whole world is arraigned (see Acts 17:31), for "all have sinned," for which the "wages" is death (Romans 3:23; 6:23).

An ancient Roman governor reacted in a very human way to Paul's sermon about this coming confrontation: "As he reasoned about righteousness, self-control, and the judgment to come, Felix was afraid" ["trembled," KJV] (Acts 24:25). And well may we tremble!

But facing reality is always a healthy choice. It is a salutary thing to anticipate this judgment, for "we must all appear" in it (2 Corinthians 5:10). And as of today, it is fortunately not too late to take constructive steps toward getting ready. To try to put the matter out of mind would be foolish, for if death and taxes are certain, this is even more so.

But This Judgment Is Good News!

We are mistaken if we have the common idea that God is a vengeful Deity waiting for a chance to zap us with His lightning bolts of retribution. Several biblical disclosures seem startlingly different from what most people suppose will be the final judgment:

1. *It was never God's plan that any of us face the terrifying prospect of facing guilty charges.* Jesus said that "everlasting fire" is specifically "prepared for the devil and his angels," not for humans (Matthew 25:41). If any human lands there, it will not be because *God* wills it, but because he himself has willed it. Nevertheless it is evident that some unfortunate

souls will participate in the devil's fate. The reason has to be that they have beaten back every effort God has made to save them from it.

2. *Jesus declares Good News in what appears to be a happy contradiction.* Not all must "appear" in condemnation. "In very truth, anyone who gives heed to what I say and puts his trust [the original words are *believe it*] in Him who sent Me has hold of eternal life, and does not come up for judgment, but has already passed from death to life" (John 5:24, NEB). The word *judgment* here means condemnation, the point being that God exempts believers from the terrible experience of facing trial.

3. *God is just, as well as merciful; therefore He has placed the judgment of human beings in the hands of One who understands the human experience.* "The Father judges no one," says Jesus, "but has committed all judgment to the Son, ... and has given Him authority to execute judgment also, because He is the Son of Man" (John 5:22-27). Christ is our Peer. No one more friendly to us could be found.

If in a human law court the judge and all the jury are your warm personal friends, you could not wish for a more favorable chance of acquittal. Yet the Son of Man will do for us what no earthly friends can do when we are in trouble. John says: "I write this to you so that you will not sin. But if anybody does sin, we have One who speaks to the Father in our defense—Jesus Christ, the Righteous One. He is the atoning sacrifice for our sins, and not only for ours but also for the sins of the whole world" (1 John 2:1, 2, NIV). Some translations say that He is our Advocate, or defense attorney.

4. *How can He be our Advocate in a law case? Here is the answer: He has already suffered the condemnation of our deserved judgment.* As the second Adam of the human race, He has adopted the human race "in Him" corporately. It is true even if we haven't known it; and it is true unless we choose to reject it. The "adoption" took place before we were born, even "from the foundation of the world" when the Lamb was "slain" for us (Revelation 13:8). Christ has given the entire human race a "verdict of acquittal" (Romans 5:16, 17, NEB). If this seems too good to be true, just consider that because Christ died for the world, God can "make His sun to rise on the evil and on the good, and sends rain on the just and on the unjust" (see Matthew 5:45). That means clearly that He treats everyone as though he or she had never sinned. Otherwise, He would be forced to let Satan zap every human being. (This is called grace.)

5. *The death that Jesus died on the cross was the ultimate degree of condemnation, for "He has made Him who knew no sin to be sin for us"* (2 Corinthians 5:21). The horror He went through was to feel "forsaken" by His Father as He "bore our sins in His own body on the tree, that we, having died to sins, might live for righteousness—by whose stripes you were healed" (1 Peter 2:24). It was in His own nervous system, in Himself, that Christ "bore" that lethal burden. The idea is that when He died, we also died, not as being half-way our own saviors, but, because as the second Adam, Christ assumed the humanity of the human race along with our liabilities. And we follow Him through faith. "*I* have been crucified with Christ," says Paul (Galatians 2:20). Whatever lightning bolts of hot divine wrath are to fall on sinners in the final judgment, they have already fallen on Christ at the cross. He took them as our Substitute.

6. *Therefore there is not the slightest reason why anyone should have to go through that experience again, unless he asks for it by rejecting this identity with Christ.* This identity of being "in Christ" is ours, if we will believe. Christ's death is far more than a legal maneuver to satisfy the statutory claims of a broken law. It is this, of course, but faith in Him involves much more. It involves our personal identifying with Him. The believing sinner *feels* himself involved "with Christ," accepts the divine judgment as being for his sins, and he actually suffers it "in Christ" through faith. Justice can make no further claims against him.

This is why he "does not come up for judgment." And "the whole world" has that advantage if they don't reject it by the sin of unbelief!

7. *It follows that the only kind of "judgment" that can take place for a believer "in Christ" is complete acquittal.* Christ promises to conduct his defense before any enemies, to refute any of their charges against him: "I will confess his name before My Father and before His angels" (Revelation 3:5). The Father is not our enemy, but we *do* have an enemy in the judgment (the word "Satan" means "enemy"). The prophet Zechariah describes the courtroom scene ("Joshua" is a symbol of all who believe):

> "Then he showed me Joshua the high priest standing before the angel of the Lord, and Satan [meaning "enemy"] standing at his right side to accuse him. The Lord said to Satan, 'The Lord rebuke you, Satan! ... Is not this man a burning stick snatched from the fire?'
>
> "Now Joshua was dressed in filthy clothes as he stood before the angel. The angel said to those who were standing before him, 'Take off his filthy clothes.'

"Then he said to Joshua, 'See, I have taken away your sin, and I will put rich garments on you'" (Zechariah 3:1-4, NIV).

Our "adversary" knows plenty about us. If he had half a chance he would force us to hang our heads in everlasting shame. But something has happened to the believer in the wonderful transaction known as justification by faith. Christ's perfect righteousness is lawfully credited to his account.

It has also transformed him to be obedient to the law of God. Since "all have sinned," no one will ever have any better title than that of "a burning stick snatched from the fire." But it's glorious Good News that such a title is legally already ours by virtue of the sacrifice of the Second Adam—subject only to our response of faith.

The "rich garments" that cover poor Joshua's nakedness of soul are the imputed (and imparted!) garment of Christ's righteousness. Revelation focuses on the same scene, for when Christ confesses before His Father the name of the overcomer, "the same shall be clothed in white raiment" (Revelation 3:5, KJV). The "adversary" is forced to hang his head in shame when the penitent's faith is mentioned, for genuine faith is heart participation "with Christ" in His crucifixion, a sharing "with Him" of death to sin in which self has been crucified "with Christ."

Satan hates the very thought, but he must respect such faith of a human who identifies with the One who conquered sin. The adversary of the human race is forever silenced.

Satan hates the cross, but if you love it, you no longer have anything to do with him. That stinging—"The Lord rebuke you, Satan!"—is a slap in his face from which he can never recover. I don't know how anyone could adequately describe the dramatic excitement of that moment in final judgment!

It's Impossible to Be Afraid of the Judgment if There Is Love (*Agape*) in Our Hearts

"Love [*agape*] has been perfected among us in this: that we may have boldness in the day of judgment. ... There is no fear in love; but perfect love casts out fear" (1 John 4:17, 18). The reason is that this kind of love (*agape*) is the point where our identification "with Christ" takes place, because His *agape* has already gone to hell and come back, and if that love dwells in our hearts, all fear is automatically expelled. The cross does it for us. In abolishing the fear of hell, all lesser fears are also overcome.

8. *Scripture makes plain that so far as believers are concerned, this triumphant vindication takes place before Christ returns.* Those who have died in Christ "sleep in Jesus" until the first resurrection (see 1 Thessalonians 4:14, 15; Revelation 20:5, 6).

There are two resurrections: "The hour is coming in which all who are in the graves will hear His voice and come forth—those who have done good, to the resurrection of life, and those who have done evil, to the resurrection of condemnation" (John 5:28, 29). The first comes at the return of Christ when He calls the sleeping saints to arise: "Blessed and holy is he who has part in the first resurrection. Over such the second death has no power" (Revelation 20:6). The second comes at the end of the 1000 years when the lost must come forth to face final executive judgment, "the resurrection of condemnation" (John 5:29; cf. Revelation 20:5).

What determines whether one comes up in the first resurrection or has to wait for the second? Jesus spoke of a pre-advent judgment when the cases of all believers will be taken up—necessarily *before* the first resurrection. Those "are counted worthy to attain that age, and the resurrection from the dead" (Luke 20:35). Such "counting" requires what some have called an "investigative judgment," a term that is meaningful in the light of Scripture teaching. All judgments must include honest investigation!

Daniel saw in vision the saints vindicated in judgment *before* the end of human history (see Daniel 7:9-14, 22, 26). Obviously, Jesus' confessing their names "before My Father and before His angels" (Revelation 3:5) must *precede* the first resurrection. "The time of the dead, that they should be judged, and that You should reward Your servants the prophets, and the saints, and those who fear Your name" occurs at the sounding of the seventh trumpet, while human life goes on and "the nations were angry" (Revelation 11:18; see also verse 15). We are living in those times today. This means that this most momentous judgment is *now in progress.*

9. *A distinct message tells "every nation, tribe, people, and tongue" that the time has come to notice what is happening* (Revelation 5:9, 7:9). "I saw another angel flying in the midst of heaven, having the everlasting gospel to preach to those who dwell on the earth … saying with a loud voice, 'Fear God and give glory to Him, for the hour of His judgment has come'" (Revelation 14:6, 7).

The import is clear: while "the nations [are] angry" and multitudes are absorbed in "eating and drinking, marrying and giving in marriage"

(Matthew 24:38), the solemn court proceedings that settle everyone's eternal destiny are being decided! The same court is settling the case in "the great controversy between Christ and Satan." God also has been on trial!

Jesus compares this time to "the days before the flood" of Noah (verse 38), when a pre-flood judgment also settled everyone's destiny with most not realizing it. Noah and his family were locked safely inside the ark for seven days, and the unbelieving multitudes were irrevocably locked outside, while they "did not know until the flood came and took them all away" (verse 39; see Genesis 7:7-12, 21).

Our judgment does not hinge primarily on our having *done* this or that, but on our *believing or disbelieving* a divine love that has given sacrificially, to an infinite degree. Sometimes in our dreams the cosmic curtain is swept back and we catch a glimpse of the reality of future judgment and of how much we need the grace of God to prepare for it. We can look forward with prophetic insight to the time of the final verdict which in truth will be pronounced by each lost soul himself. For us to be able to catch a glimpse of this now, is good news to be profoundly thankful for.

In the day of final judgment, every lost soul will understand how he came to reject truth. He will "see" the cross, and its real bearing will be seen by every mind that has been blinded by the love of sin. Before Calvary with its mysterious Victim, sinners will see themselves condemned. Every one of their lying excuses will be swept away. His sin will appear in its heinous character. People will see what their choice has been. Every question of truth and error in the long-standing "controversy" will then be made plain. In the judgment of the universe, God will stand clear of blame for the existence or continuance of evil. It will be demonstrated there was no defect in God's government, no cause for rebellion to arise and be supported.

10. *The "Good News" is far better than we may have thought.* Not only is it possible for us to make a right choice *today*, but the mighty Holy Spirit makes it easy for us to make that right choice. It will lead to the fulfillment of every glorious dream we have had since childhood. To be at one with God is to be at one with the light and life and love of the vast universe that He has created.

Heaven's Day of Atonement

Even now devout Jews celebrate Yom Kippur as a solemn day of judgment. In the ancient Hebrew sanctuary service, the Day of

Atonement was the occasion when the righteous and the wicked were separated in judgment (see Leviticus 23:27-30). The entire Hebrew sanctuary ministry was symbolic of the work of the heavenly High Priest, Christ (see Hebrews 8:1-5; 4:14-16). The typical Day of Atonement was also symbolic of the final period of preadvent judgment that determines who of the sleeping dead will arise in the first resurrection, and who must await the dreaded second resurrection. It will also decide who among the living in the last days will "be counted worthy to escape all these things that will come to pass, and to stand before the Son of Man" (Luke 21:36).

Solemn thought! We are living in that time *now*.

The Good News is that that Judge is your Brother "in the flesh," the Son of Man who took upon Himself "the likeness of sinful flesh" and knows exactly how "in all points" we are tempted. "In that He Himself has suffered being tempted, He is able to aid those who are tempted" (Romans 8:3; Hebrews 4:15; 2:18).

He doesn't have to persuade the Father to accept you, for "the Father Himself loves you," He says (John 16:27). He doesn't have to persuade those millions of angels to be on your side, for they are already "ministering spirits sent forth to minister for those who will inherit salvation" (Hebrews 1:14). He doesn't have to buy off the devil, because Christ has met the demands of justice at Calvary. So who in this judgment does He have to persuade in your behalf?

You are the key figure in this drama who needs help, who needs to be persuaded of something. Your first step is to *believe* the Good News of God's grace, which is infinitely better than you have thought it to be.

The result of such believing is that you are reconciled to God; all the misunderstandings about Him are cleared up. This is receiving the atonement, exactly the right thing to do in this grand heavenly Day of Atonement.

Right Now Is When You Decide

God knows that once you *believe* the good news, your faith will manifest itself immediately, for "faith work[s] through love" (Galatians 5:6). As sunshine is filtered through the prism to produce those glorious colors of the spectrum from infrared to violet, so the faith of Christ shining out from your heart finds prismatic display in your life of obedience to all His commandments.

The devil will say, "Impossible!"

I plead with you, *believe* that it *is* possible. Silence him.

Such genuine New Testament faith means indescribably sweet reconciliation with God, peace of heart, harmony with God's family, and eternal life. Neither you nor I deserve one iota of it, but Someone who risked everything purchased it for us.

We can *never* say a big enough Thank You to Him!

Your Personal Notes

The Ancient of Days came, and a judgment was made in favor of the saints of the Most High, and the time came for the saints to possess the kingdom ... The saints of the Most High shall receive the kingdom, and possess the kingdom forever, even forever and ever (Daniel 7:22; 18).

Appendix A

Though Russell H. Conwell's *Acres of Diamonds* was spread all over the United States in the late nineteenth century, time and its cares have made the lesson presented in this lecture more valuable for thoughtful people today. We reproduce it here to enrich the multitudes who read this book. Conwell was an American Baptist minister, orator, philanthropist, lawyer, and writer who preached for more than fifty years. As a young man, studying law at Yale University, he delivered his first platform lecture as the Civil War (1861-65) was dragging on with all its passions, patriotism, horrors, and fears. Considering everything, the most remarkable thing in Russell Conwell's remarkable life is this lecture, "Acres of Diamonds"— that is, the lecture itself, the number of times he delivered it (thousands of times), and what a source of inspiration it has been to myriads of young people. His famous lecture is reproduced here, in part, to supplement the message found in Chapter 9 of this little book of *Good News*.

"Acres of Diamonds"

When going down the Tigris and Euphrates rivers many years ago with a party of English travelers I found myself under the direction of an old Arab guide whom we hired up at Bagdad, and I have often thought how that guide resembled our barbers in certain mental characteristics. He thought that it was not only his duty to guide us down those rivers, and do what he was paid for doing, but also to entertain us with stories curious and weird, ancient and modern, strange and familiar. Many of them I have forgotten, and I am glad I have, but there is one I shall never forget.

The old guide was leading my camel by its halter along the banks of those ancient rivers, and he told me story after story until I grew weary of his story-telling and ceased to listen. I have never been irritated with that guide when he lost his temper as I ceased listening. But I remember that he took off his Turkish cap and swung it in a circle to get my attention. I could see it through the corner of my eye, but I determined not to look straight at him for fear he would tell another story. But although I am not a woman, I did finally look, and as soon as I did he went right into another story.

Said he, "I will tell you a story now which I reserve for my particular friends." When he emphasized the words "particular friends," I listened, and I have ever been glad I did. I really feel devoutly thankful, that there are 1,674 young men who have been carried through college by this lecture who are also glad that I did listen. The old guide told me that there once lived not far from the River Indus an ancient Persian by the name of Ali Hafed. He said that Ali Hafed owned a very large farm, that he had orchards, grain-fields, and gardens; that he had money at interest, and was a wealthy and contented man. He was contented because he was wealthy, and wealthy because he was contented. One day there visited that old Persian farmer one of these ancient Buddhist priests, one of the wise men of the East. He sat down by the fire and told the old farmer how this world of ours was made. He said that this world was once a mere bank of fog, and that the Almighty thrust His finger into this bank of fog, and began slowly to move His finger around, increasing the speed until at last He whirled this bank of fog into a solid ball of fire. Then it went rolling through the universe, burning its way through other banks of fog, and condensed the moisture without, until it fell in floods of rain upon its hot surface, and cooled the outward crust. Then the internal fires bursting outward through the crust threw up the mountains and hills, the valleys, the plains and prairies of this wonderful world of ours. If this internal molten mass came bursting out and cooled very quickly it became granite; less quickly copper, less quickly silver, less quickly gold, and, after gold, diamonds were made.

Said the old priest, "A diamond is a congealed drop of sunlight." Now that is literally scientifically true, that a diamond is an actual deposit of carbon from the sun. The old priest told Ali Hafed that if he had one diamond the size of his thumb he could purchase the county, and if he had a mine of diamonds he could place his children upon thrones through the influence of their great wealth.

Ali Hafed heard all about diamonds, how much they were worth, and went to his bed that night a poor man. He had not lost anything, but he was poor because he was discontented, and discontented because he feared he was poor. He said, "I want a mine of diamonds," and he lay awake all night.

Early in the morning he sought out the priest. I know by experience that a priest is very cross when awakened early in the morning, and when he shook that old priest out of his dreams, Ali Hafed said to him:

"Will you tell me where I can find diamonds?"

"Diamonds! What do you want with diamonds?" "Why, I wish to be immensely rich." "Well, then, go along and find them. That is all you have to do; go and find them, and then you have them." "But I don't know where to go." "Well, if you will find a river that runs through white sands, between high mountains, in those white sands you will always find diamonds." "I don't believe there is any such river." "Oh yes, there are plenty of them. All you have to do is to go and find them, and then you have them." Said Ali Hafed, "I will go."

So he sold his farm, collected his money, left his family in charge of a neighbor, and away he went in search of diamonds. He began his search, very properly to my mind, at the Mountains of the Moon. Afterward he came around into Palestine, then wandered on into Europe, and at last when his money was all spent and he was in rags, wretchedness, and poverty, he stood on the shore of that bay at Barcelona, in Spain, when a great tidal wave came rolling in between the pillars of Hercules, and the poor, afflicted, suffering, dying man could not resist the awful temptation to cast himself into that incoming tide, and he sank beneath its foaming crest, never to rise in this life again.

When that old guide had told me that awfully sad story he stopped the camel I was riding on and went back to fix the baggage that was coming off another camel, and I had an opportunity to muse over his story while he was gone. I remember saying to myself, "Why did he reserve that story for his `particular friends'?" There seemed to be no beginning, no middle, no end, nothing to it. That was the first story I had ever heard told in my life, and would be the first one I ever read, in which the hero was killed in the first chapter. I had but one chapter of that story, and the hero was dead.

When the guide came back and took up the halter of my camel, he went right ahead with the story, into the second chapter, just as though there had been no break. The man who purchased Ali Hafed's farm one day led his camel into the garden to drink, and as that camel put its nose into the shallow water of that garden brook, Ali Hafed's successor noticed a curious flash of light from the white sands of the stream. He pulled out a black stone having an eye of light reflecting all the hues of the rainbow. He took the pebble into the house and put it on the mantel which covers the central fires, and forgot all about it.

A few days later this same old priest came in to visit Ali Hafed's successor, and the moment he opened that drawing-room door he saw that flash of light on the mantel, and he rushed up to it, and shouted: "Here is a diamond! Has Ali Hafed returned?"

"Oh no, Ali Hafed has not returned, and that is not a diamond. That is nothing but a stone we found right out here in our own garden."

"But," said the priest, "I tell you I know a diamond when I see it. I know positively that is a diamond."

Then together they rushed out into that old garden and stirred up the white sands with their fingers, and lo! there came up other more beautiful and valuable gems than the first. "Thus," said the guide to me, and, friends, it is historically true, "was discovered the diamond mine of Golconda, the most magnificent diamond mine in all the history of mankind, excelling the Kimberly itself. The *Kohinoor*, and the *Orloff* of the crown jewels of England and Russia, the largest on earth, came from that mine."

When that old Arab guide told me the second chapter of his story, he then took off his Turkish cap and swung it around in the air again to get my attention to the moral. Those Arab guides have morals to their stories, although they are not always moral. As he swung his hat, he said to me, "Had Ali Hafed remained at home and dug in his own cellar, or underneath his own wheat fields, or in his own garden, instead of wretchedness, starvation, and death by suicide in a strange land, he would have had 'acres of diamonds.' For every acre of that old farm, yes, every shovelful, afterward revealed gems which since have decorated the crowns of monarchs."

When he had added the moral to his story I saw why he reserved it for "his particular friends." But I did not tell him I could see it. It was that mean old Arab's way of going around a thing like a lawyer, to say indirectly what he did not dare say directly, that "in his private opinion there was a certain young man then traveling down the Tigris River that might better be at home in America." I did not tell him I could see that, but I told him his story reminded *me* of one, and I told it to him quick, and I think I will tell it to you.

I told him of a man out in California in 1847 who owned a ranch. He heard they had discovered gold in southern California, and so with a passion for gold he sold his ranch to Colonel Sutter, and away he went, never to come back. Colonel Sutter put a mill upon a stream that ran through that ranch, and one day his little girl brought some wet sand from the raceway into their home and sifted it through her fingers before the fire, and in that falling sand a visitor saw the first shining scales of real gold that were ever discovered in California.

The man who had owned that ranch wanted gold, and he could have secured it for the mere taking. Indeed, thirty-eight millions of dollars has been taken out of a very few acres since then. About eight years ago I delivered this lecture in a city that stands on that farm, and they told me that a one-third owner for years and years had been getting one hundred and twenty dollars in gold every fifteen minutes, sleeping or waking, without taxation. You and I would enjoy an income like that— if we didn't have to pay an income tax.

But a better illustration really than that occurred here in our own Pennsylvania. If there is anything I enjoy above another on the platform, it is to get one of these German audiences in Pennsylvania before me, and fire that at them, and I enjoy it to-night. There was a man living in Pennsylvania, not unlike some Pennsylvanians you have seen, who owned a farm, and he did with that farm just what I should do with a farm if I owned one in Pennsylvania—he sold it.

But before he sold it he decided to secure employment collecting coal-oil for his cousin, who was in the business in Canada, where they first discovered oil on this continent. They dipped it from the running streams at that early time.

So this Pennsylvania farmer wrote to his cousin asking for employment. You see, friends, this farmer was not altogether a foolish man. No, he was not. He did not leave his farm until he had something else to do. (Of all the simpletons the stars shine on I don't know of a worse one than the man who leaves one job before he has gotten another. That has especial reference to my profession, and has no reference whatever to a man seeking a divorce!) When he wrote to his cousin for employment, his cousin replied, "I cannot engage you because you know nothing about the oil business."

Well, then the old farmer said, "I *will* know," and with most commendable zeal (characteristic of the students of Temple University) he set himself at the study of the whole subject. He began away back at the second day of God's creation when this world was covered thick and deep with that rich vegetation which since has turned to the primitive beds of coal. He studied the subject until he found that the draining really of those rich beds of coal furnished the coal-oil that was worth pumping, and then he found how it came up with the living springs. He studied until he knew what it looked like, smelled like, tasted like, and how to refine it. Now said he in his letter to his cousin, "I understand the oil business." His cousin answered, "All right, come on."

So he sold his farm, according to the county record, for $833 (even money, "no cents"). He had scarcely gone from that place before the man who purchased the spot went out to arrange for the watering of the cattle. He found the previous owner had gone out years before and put a plank across the brook back of the barn, edgewise into the surface of the water just a few inches. The purpose of that plank at that sharp angle across the brook was to throw over to the other bank a dreadful-looking scum through which the cattle would not put their noses. But with that plank there to throw it all over to one side, the cattle would drink below, and thus that man who had gone to Canada had been himself damming back for twenty-three years a flood of coal-oil which the state geologists of Pennsylvania declared to us ten years later was even then worth a hundred millions of dollars to our state, and four years ago our geologist declared the discovery to be worth to our state a thousand millions of dollars. The man who owned that territory on which the city of Titusville now stands, and those Pleasantville valleys, had studied the subject from the second day of God's creation clear down to the present time. He studied it until he knew all about it, and yet he is said to have sold the whole of it for $833, and again I say, "no *sense*."

But I need another illustration. I found it in Massachusetts, and I am sorry I did because that is the state I came from. This young man in Massachusetts furnishes just another phase of my thought. He went to Yale College and studied mines and mining, and became such an adept as a mining engineer that he was employed by the authorities of the university to train students who were behind their classes. During his senior year he earned $15 a week for doing that work.[1] When he graduated they raised his pay from $15 to $45 a week, and offered him a professorship, and as soon as they did he went right home to his mother.

If they had raised that boy's pay from $15 to $15.60 he would have stayed and been proud of the place, but when they put it up to $45 at one leap, he said, "Mother, I won't work for $45 a week. The idea of a man with a brain like mine working for $45 a week! Let's go out in California and stake out gold-mines and silver-mines, and be immensely rich."

Said his mother, "Now, Charlie, it is just as well to be happy as it is to be rich."

"Yes," said Charlie, "but it is just as well to be rich and happy, too." And they were both right about it. As he was an only son and she a widow, of course he had his way. They always do.

They sold out in Massachusetts, and instead of going to California they went to Wisconsin, where he went into the employ of the Superior Copper Mining Company at $15 a week again, but with the proviso

1. To add some perspective, the average wage for a common working man in 1890 in Central Pennsylvania was $3/day. A sampling of the cost of goods reveals the following (food prices are per pound): sugar 8¢; rice 9¢; wheat 99½¢; oats 60¢; beef roast 15¢; eggs 25¢ (dozen). Kerosene used for lighting was 18¢ per gallon, and an ordinary shovel cost 50¢ at the hardware store.

in his contract that he should have an interest in any mines he should discover for the company.

I don't believe he ever discovered a mine, and if I am looking in the face of any stockholder of that copper company you wish he had discovered something or other. I have friends who are not here because they could not afford a ticket, who did have stock in that company at the time this young man was employed there. This young man went out there, and I have not heard a word from him. I don't know what became of him, and I don't know whether he found any mines or not, but I don't believe he ever did.

But I do know the other end of the line. He had scarcely gotten out of the old homestead before the succeeding owner went out to dig potatoes. The potatoes were already growing in the ground when he bought the farm, and as the old farmer was bringing in a basket of potatoes it hugged very tight between the ends of the stone fence. You know in Massachusetts our farms are nearly all stone wall. There you are obliged to be very economical of front gateways in order to have some place to put the stone. When that basket hugged so tight he set it down on the ground, and then dragged on one side, and pulled on the other side, and as he was dragging that basket through this farmer noticed in the upper and outer corner of that stone wall, right next the gate, a block of native silver eight inches square.

That professor of mines, mining, and mineralogy who knew so much about the subject that he would not work for $45 a week, when he sold that homestead in Massachusetts, sat right on that silver to make the bargain. He was born on that homestead, was brought up there, and had gone back and forth rubbing the stone with his sleeve until it reflected is countenance, and seemed to say, "Here is a hundred thousand dollars right down here just for the taking." But he would not take it. It was in a home in Newburyport, Massachusetts, and there was no silver there, all away off—well, I don't know where, and he did not, but somewhere else, and he was a professor of mineralogy.

Appendix A was excerpted from the lecture "Acres of Diamonds" given by Russell H. Conwell (1843-1925). Conwell was founder and first president of Temple University, Philadelphia, PA. *Acres of Diamonds* was first published in book form in 1890 by the John Y. Huber Co. of Philadelphia. Sourced from Project Gutenberg EBook: https://www.gutenberg.org/files/368/368-h/368-h.htm

Your Personal Notes

"Again, the kingdom of heaven is like treasure hidden in a field, which a man found and hid; and for joy over it he goes and sells all that he has and buys that field. "Again, the kingdom of heaven is like a merchant seeking beautiful pearls, who, when he had found one pearl of great price, went and sold all that he had and bought it (Matthew 13:44-46).

Robert J. Wieland

1916-2011

As a boy, Robert J. Wieland read avidly and widely, and developed his growing writing talent. Listening to an old cracked Victrola recording of Jascha Heifetz started a lifetime of violin playing and a passion for classical music.

After graduating from the seminary at Emmanuel Missionary College near Washington, D.C., he became the pastor of a small church in St. Augustine, Florida. It was in Florida where he met Grace, which began 66 years of a devoted, loving, and supportive marriage that inspired and nurtured all those around them until Grace's death in 2008.

In 1945 they, and their young family of three, answered a call to become missionaries in Uganda, where Elder Wieland planted churches and a hospital that survived the Idi Amin regime. It was there that he discovered that in order to hold the people in the church the people needed to grasp the "most precious" truths of "Christ and Him crucified." This became the signature of his ministry and writings.

In 1952 the family moved to Nairobi, Kenya, where he was a pastor, church administrator, radio speaker, editor, and prolific writer. He was fluent in Luganda and Swahili, and many Africans still read his materials and remember him and Grace with love and appreciation.

After returning to the United States he pastored churches in California, and he and Grace retired there. But retirement was not in his "vocabulary" as he continued into his 90s to give seminars, and write articles and books. In order to share the Good News with a wider audience, he authored "Dial Daily Bread," an inspiring daily devotional message, the e-mail version of which is continuing into its 22nd year. (To subscribe, write to dailybread@1888message.org.)

Publications by Robert J. Wieland
(A Partial List)

Books

Powerful Good News

In Search of the Cross: Learning to "Glory" in It

A New Look at God's Law: How the Ten Commandments Become Good News

The Gospel in Revelation (a verse-by-verse study)

The Gospel in Daniel (a verse-by-verse-study)

Ephesians—You've Been "Adopted": Paul's "Most Precious" Letter Verse-by-Verse

Mary Magdalene, The Woman the World Can Never Forget: The Bible Story

Gold Tried in the Fire: Re-discovering the Powerful Bible Idea of What Dynamic Faith Is

In Search of the Treasure of Faith

The Lion That Ran Away: Children's Stories From Africa ... and Other Places

Pamphlets and Other Publications

The Nearness of Your Savior

Taking the Deadlock Out of Wedlock

The Lady Who Said "Yes" to God

The Word That Turned the World Upside Down

The Backward Prayer

Islam Challenges the World